Kathleen Owens, PhD
President

Date: _12-4-12_

TO: _Lisa Mc Garry_

_____

_____

_____

☐ For Your Comments   ☐ Please Handle

☑ For Your Information   ☐ Keep or Discard

☐ For Your Approval   ☑ Take Appropriate Action

☐ Call Me   ☐ Reply & Send Me Copy

☐ See Me   ☐ For Your Signature

See related email
message...

NOLAN, IDA
AND
CINDY
—
The son, daughter and wife of my dreams.

TABLE OF CONTENTS

INTRODUCTION

Contrary to popular belief, most sports broadcasters are really not living their dream. Almost every one of us who is fortunate enough to turn our passions into a profession started out wanting to be the star quarterback or the 20-win pitcher or to win Wimbledon or the Masters Golf Championship. At 10 or 12 years old, we swished a 15-foot jump shot and envisioned it capturing the NCAA Tournament.

Even if we achieved success on various levels very few of us had the incredible talent it takes to turn athleticism into a profession. That being the case, we turned to the next best thing. Not only that, we picked a career we can practice for the rest of our lives.

Being a sportscaster is everything I ever dreamed it could be. Many "glamour" jobs are nowhere nearly as glamorous as they appear to outsiders. This one is even more glamorous. There's one catch. These jobs are hard to get. They're highly competitive and often require years of preparation.

Few play-by-play broadcasters describe the games of the teams they rooted for while growing up. This is one field where you have to be willing to move. Often the young broadcaster must start at a very small station for minimum pay. The trail to the top jobs is long and filled with disappointments. Only the most driven, resilient, dedicated people survive, but those who achieve their goal have something very special.

I decided to write this book for those who would like to focus on some of the basics involved in the various aspects of sports broadcasting. It is not meant as a substitute for a formal education. While there may be a few exceptions, most successful broadcasters have college degrees.

Today most universities have communications departments complete with student operated radio and television stations where prospective broadcasters can gain valuable experience.

One other piece of advice before delving into the basics of sportscasting. Young people should learn all they can about the various parts of their profession. Limiting yourself to sports is a mistake. In the first place, few small stations hire somebody to do just sports. Young broadcasters have to be prepared to handle a large variety of assignments. Also in a field this competitive, it is a mistake to be too specialized. Leave your avenues open and you'll never be sorry.

The other advantage in pursuing communications in college is the opportunity to take a wide variety of courses not connected with sports or broadcasting. The best broadcasters are well rounded with knowledge in a lot of other areas. It may not seem it at the time, but courses in literature, history, political science, and psychology will all play an important role in your career growth. The best way to develop an exceptional vocabulary is through reading. I'd bet anything that the broadcasters who you most admire for their descriptive abilities are voracious readers.

While I've broadcast many sports, my greatest area of concentration has been football. For over 30 years, I've been the play-by-play voice of the Philadelphia Eagles. My basics in football are the result of the theories I've developed over the years.

For baseball, basketball, hockey, radio sports talk, interviewing techniques, nightly television anchoring, and public address announcing, I've turned to friends who have achieved great success in those areas. These people are respected throughout the country and their words will give you a blueprint for a solid foundation in their areas of sports broadcasting.

TELEVISION VS. RADIO

The play-by-play fundamentals I'm about to describe are developed for radio. I am convinced that any skilled radio play-by-play person can easily adapt to television. For someone who has only done television the transition to radio is not nearly as easy. Almost all of the outstanding telecasters have radio play-by-play in their background.

Regardless of the sport, the radio play-by-play person paints a picture. That picture includes not only a description of the action but a feel for the ambiance that the spectators at the event are experiencing. The color analyst drops in from time to time to add expertise or some personal information about the competitors but the play-by-play person is the dominant member of the radio broadcast.

On television the play-by-play broadcaster's job is to caption the picture and set the scene. The color analyst has the more dominant role in a sports telecast.

There are television color analysts in almost every sport who have become major stars because of their unique personalities. Some are controversial – fans love them or hate them. Dick Vitale, a former coach, is as much a part of college basketball as the cheerleaders. His expressions such as "He's a P-T-P – a prime time player" are known to every follower of the game. When he enters an arena there's a big reaction from the crowd. At the same time there are viewers who would rather hear chalk screech on a blackboard than listen to Vitale's less than soothing delivery.

The most recognized color analyst in the NFL over the past three decades has been former Oakland Raiders coach John Madden. Madden retired in April 2009 because he wanted to spend more time with his family. His aversion to air travel forced him to move across the country by bus, "The Madden Cruiser". For six months a year he was rarely at his California home. On the air Madden came through as "the guy next door". In this case, however, the guy next door had a wealth of football knowledge and the ability to explain the most technical aspects of the game in a way that any fan could understand.

When he was paired with Pat Summerall on CBS, Summerall merely set up the play and let Madden be Madden. On Monday Night Football on ABC and most recently on Sunday Night Football on NBC he worked with Al Michaels. Michaels interjected his own personality into the broadcast and that also meshed extremely well with Madden.

Madden was a master at using the telestrator to diagram plays on the screen. On Thanksgiving games he even used this device to demonstrate the carving of a turducken – a turkey stuffed with a duck stuffed with a chicken. His video game "John Madden Football" has made millions of dollars and has educated millions of fans about football strategy.

In its most basic form here is an example illustrating the difference between radio and television play-by-play.

Radio: *"First and ten for the Eagles – the ball on their own 35. They break the huddle. Kevin Kolb up and under center. The backs are in the "I" formation. The wide receivers are split. Now Brent Celek comes in motion from right to left. Kolb takes the snap. He's looking down field. He fires. Complete to Celek. He's at midfield – down to the 45 – the 40 and finally brought down by LaRon Landry at the 35. That's a gain of 30 yards."*

Television: "*First and ten for the Eagles on their 35. That's Celek in motion to the top of your screen. Kolb to pass – Celek at midfield – down at the 35 – LaRon Landry on the tackle – 30 yards on the play.*"

Too many telecasters still insist on doing radio play-by-play which can be very annoying.

Making the adjustment is not difficult. It's something every radio broadcaster should be able to do.

In baseball quite a few broadcasters switch back and forth between radio and TV in the same game. The really good ones are cognizant of the switch and adapt their delivery.

FOOTBALL

Merrill Reese and Mike Quick

THE SET UP

I always arrive at the stadium several hours before the kick off. I carry a book filled with notes that I've prepared during the week. Many of those notes may never get used, but I subscribe to the theory of "over prepare – under deliver."

I watch the warm-ups very carefully and actually write down the range that the kickers display in each direction. I know that from my left to my right David Akers on this day is clearing the cross bar from 52 yards. In the opposite direction his effective range may be only 48 yards.

I also focus on the punters to see how the wind in each direction is affecting the flight of the football. When the teams warm up I focus my binoculars on any player whose status was questionable before the game. If LeSean McCoy has missed practice sessions during the week I want to see how he's moving today.

I open my notebook to a page with topics I plan to discuss with my color analyst before the game begins. While this isn't scripted, there is still a strong outline necessary for a comprehensive pre-game discussion.

At the bottom of the page I include three boxes that are to be checked off as I mention the names of the officials, describe the uniforms and indicate the directions which each team will move in the first quarter. By drawing the small boxes I eliminate the possibility of forgetting to mention any of these three important things.

The officials play a very important role and should always be identified before the game. You are painting a picture so it is important for listeners to know that the Eagles are wearing their midnight green jerseys and white pants and that the Steelers are wearing their white jerseys with black numbers, gold pants and black helmets.

The directions come after the coin toss when you can point out which team won the toss and what they decided.

Example: *"The Eagles have won the toss and have elected to receive. In the first quarter they'll be moving from left to right." This aids the listeners in visualizing the game action.*

Having a good spotter is a tremendous help to the football play-by-play broadcaster.

The spotter sits next to the play-by-play broadcaster and sets up two spotting boards. These boards contain the numbers, names and vital information about the players on each team. They're also set up in a basic formation and provide a depth chart.

The spotter places a colored thumb tack next to the names of the players who are on the field at that moment. There is a separate board for each team. Both sides are utilized. The Eagles offense is on one side and the defense on the other. The same for the opposition.

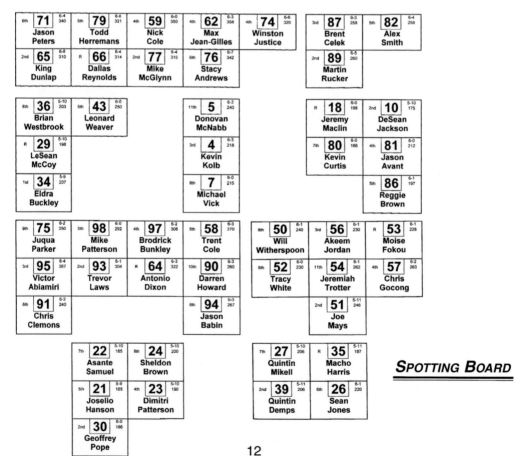

SPOTTING BOARD

While the broadcaster should have the names and numbers of the quarterbacks, running backs, tight ends, and wide receivers memorized, the spotter points to the player with the ball and the player or players involved in the tackle.

When the broadcaster follows the play downfield it is also helpful if the spotter can be aware of other factors involved during a play. By prearranged hand signals he can indicate who rushed the passer or who deflected the ball or which lineman forced the ball carrier into the grasp of the tackler.

HAND SIGNALS

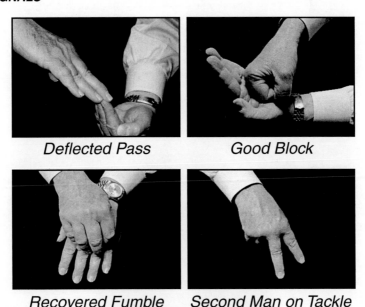

Deflected Pass   Good Block

Recovered Fumble   Second Man on Tackle

Injured Player

In the NFL detailed statistics are instantly available by internet which the statistician can copy and slide across to the commentators.

If that isn't the case, the stat person should keep a running total of the following things:

1.   Carries and yardage by backs
2.   Attempts, completions, yardage, touchdowns and interceptions by the quarterbacks.
3.   Receivers – catches and yardage totals
4.   Punts and punting average
5.   Sacks
6.   Penalties and penalty yards for each team

Those are the basics.

If possible –

1.   Time of possession of each team.
2.   3rd down conversions.
3.   Number of running plays and number of passing plays.

It is also helpful if the statistician can quickly tabulate the yardage gained after a long run or reception. You must also be aware of any team or individual records that could possibly be broken during the course of the game.

GAME TIME

S.T.D.D. - Remember those letters. That's my formula. S.T.D.D. Those letters stand for Score, Time, Down, and Distance. Those are the most important elements in a football broadcast.

Fans often compliment football broadcasters on their exciting touchdown calls. Certainly a scoring play described clearly with the right amount of emotion transmitted can be memorable. But touchdown calls, alone, do not define a good football play-by-play broadcaster.

It has always been my goal to make certain that at all times the listeners are aware of the score and the time remaining in the quarters, half, game or overtime. My producer, Joe McPeak, stands behind us in the broadcast booth and if he hasn't heard me announce the score and time for two minutes he holds up a card with large letters saying SCORE/TIME and I immediately mention those two things. That's two minutes in real time – not football time which can take much longer.

The down and the distance should be mentioned before every play along with the line of scrimmage. There are no exceptions. To set up a play I might say *"It's 2nd and 4 for the Eagles with the ball on their own 36 yard line."* Then before describing the formation I may add *"They lead 7-0 with 7 minutes and 12 seconds remaining in the 1st quarter."*

If you follow these fundamentals at least the listeners will be aware of the game's status at all times.

Next it is the broadcaster's job to describe the formation. I recommend that all prospective broadcasters read some books on the technical side of football. It's not necessary to understand all of the nuances of a "West Coast" offense or of a "cover 2" defense but it is important to recognize what a team is doing when they get into formation at the line of scrimmage. I have always attended as many practices as possible. When there was something I didn't recognize or understand I made a note and made certain to ask a coach about it after practice. In this job it is very important to develop as many good relationships with coaches and players as possible. There are several assistant coaches I know to whom I can go to for information that will help me present an accurate picture of a formation.

A basic description might be something like this: *"Kevin Kolb sets up in the shotgun with McCoy and Weaver on either side. They've got 3 wide receivers with Jackson and Maclin split and Avant slotted to Maclin's left."*

That may seem like a lot to describe but it's something that I've seen over and over. Often while at practice I'll stand quietly off to the side and do play-by-play in my head as they line up. I try to come up with the description that can give the listeners the clearest possible picture.

Next I describe everything that happens – sometimes on both sides of the ball before the ball is actually snapped.
"The Cardinals are in a nickel defense – the linebackers are jump-ing around – they could be coming with the blitz. Kolb goes into a long count. Avant goes in motion to the far side."

Once the quarterback gets the ball I simply describe what I see.

"Kolb's looking down field – he floats it to Jackson – Jackson catches it at the Cardinals' 48 and is pulled down at the 46."

ADDITIONAL TIPS

Emotion: It is permissible to allow your voice to convey emotion. That contributes to an exciting broadcast. Unless you're doing a network broadcast where total impartiality is necessary it is ok to angle your coverage towards the home team. Just as a Philadelphia newspaper will inform its readers why the Eagles won or lost, you can give the score by saying, *"The Eagles lead the Giants 14-7,"* or *"The Eagles trail the Giants 14-7."*

Your voice can rise or fall with the team's performance within reason. Never get so emotional that you lose control during a play. At all times your description must remain clear. There's nothing more frustrating for a listener than to hear a broadcaster screaming before the play is completed. Describe every aspect of the action before going into superlatives.

Another thing, and this is a cardinal rule: Never, never, never use the word "we" when referring to the team that you cover. Saying "we" will kill any trace of trying to present an accurate, objective account of the game! It's fun and entertaining to capture the euphoria that surrounds a dramatic victory but don't allow yourself to become a fan. There's an old adage that says coaches who listen to the fans are soon sitting with them. It's the same for play-by-play broadcasters. Respect the fans, communicate with the fans, but keep at least a degree of professional objectivity.

Focus: During the action your eyes should be focused on the field at all times. That seems pretty obvious doesn't it? The truth is that every one of us has been caught looking away at the start of a play at some point in our careers. When that happens disaster ensues. You might be looking at your spotter or at a note from your statistician and when you turn back the actions is underway. Trying to locate the ball at this point is almost impossible.

When you look away for information between plays keep it very, very brief. Tell your spotter to point quickly to the field if he sees the team break the huddle.

Develop a technique so that during a play you can glance to the side, out of the corner of your eyes for a bit of vital information. During an interception return my spotter will often lift the board and place it in a position where I can pick up a name while still focusing on the field.

Once in Dallas, where we sit very high and very far from the field, an Eagle came up with a last second interception in the corner of the end zone. There were two Cowboys standing directly in front of him blocking my view of his number. I've learned how to bide my time if I have to until I can come up with the proper identification.

"Intercepted – intercepted by the Eagles," I exclaimed, "coming out of the end zone to the 5- 10 -15 yard line," I continued. At that point I glanced over at my spotter who had his binoculars focused on the field. I then spun back to the field and I saw a green shirted number 23 racing down the sideline. "Troy Vincent," I said confidently, "Troy Vincent with the ball. He's at the 45, 40, 35, 30, 25, 20, 15, 10, 5, touchdown – touchdown Troy Vincent – Vincent with a 105 yard interception return. The Eagles win the game!"

Sounds great, right? Uh, no! Not quite. What actually happened was that linebacker James Willis actually intercepted the ball. When I turned for a second to look at my spotter, Willis lateralled the ball to Troy Vincent who did the rest. During the replay I noticed my mistake and boy was I embarrassed. I could only admit my mistake after which I reconstructed the play for our audience.

So take it from me, keep your eyes on the field, except between plays and even then only for a few seconds. Once the play begins don't even allow yourself to blink.

Binoculars: Binoculars are a must for football broadcasters, even in the best circumstances. At some stadiums in the NFL the broadcast booths provide excellent vantage points. Philadelphia, New York, Baltimore, New England, Chicago, Cincinnati, and Seattle are among the best.

Others are only ok. Stadiums like Heinz Field in Pittsburgh and University of Phoenix Stadium in Glendale, Arizona have the booths located near the end zone which makes it difficult when the teams are at the opposite ends of the field. And then there's Washington. When Jack Kent Cook built the stadium the booth was located at midfield. When Daniel Snyder purchased the team he moved visiting radio into a corner of the end zone. The booth is also low. When players cross the 50 yard line moving away from us it's impossible to tell whether a running play gained 5 yards or 15 until the ball is spotted. The only hope is to use the binoculars. We do have a television monitor but the feeds are delayed by several seconds which puts the picture out of sync with the live action.

Under normal circumstances do not use the binoculars when the team lines up for a play. If they are far away in a goal line situation that's different. But the second the quarterback cocks his arm to pass, pull the binoculars down. You can not follow a pass play with binoculars. They're great when the ball is fumbled and you can focus on the pile. They're excellent for focusing on the ball when the officials stretch the chains to measure for a first down. Binoculars are fine for zeroing in on an injured player to provide an identification.

For the spotter the binoculars can be used on every play. For the color analyst they're worth their weight in gold. Our color analyst, former Eagles all pro wide receiver Mike Quick, will occasionally focus his binoculars on action away from the ball. He'll follow the offensive linemen for a play or two and then deliver his observations. He may focus on the wide receivers so that he can evaluate the routes that they're running. For the play-by-play broadcaster, however, the use must be very selective.

Don't jump the gun: Like top athletes in any sport the play-by-play broadcaster must learn to be patient and practice discipline.

Don't jump to conclusions. If a running back glides into the end zone for an obvious touchdown that's one thing. But if he dives for the pylon at the goal line and you're not 100% certain that he scored, wait until the official on the play either raises both arms skyward or signals that the player did not get in. It's important that you understand and are able to instantly recognize all of the officials' hand signals.

It is perfectly alright to speculate before a signal is indicated but don't be definitive. There's nothing wrong with saying, "He looks as if he picked up the first down - the officials are calling for a measurement," or "He sneaks annnnd - (official signals) he's in. Touchdown!"

Another spot where this is extremely important is on kicks – all kicks. From a sideline view it is practically impossible to tell if a field goal has been converted. You can judge the distance. You can tell if it's got the height, but because of parallax you often are unable to accurately judge the direction. Wait until the officials on the goal line give the signal.

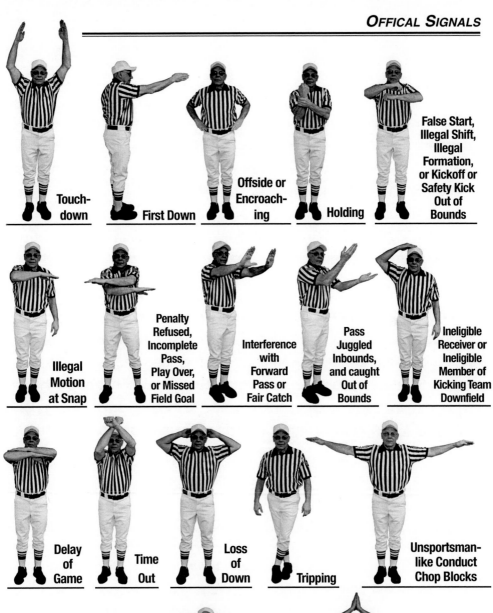

Touch-down

First Down

Offside or Encroaching

Holding

False Start, Illegal Shift, Illegal Formation, or Kickoff or Safety Kick Out of Bounds

Illegal Motion at Snap

Penalty Refused, Incomplete Pass, Play Over, or Missed Field Goal

Interference with Forward Pass or Fair Catch

Pass Juggled Inbounds, and caught Out of Bounds

Ineligible Receiver or Ineligible Member of Kicking Team Downfield

Delay of Game

Time Out

Loss of Down

Tripping

Unsportsman-like Conduct Chop Blocks

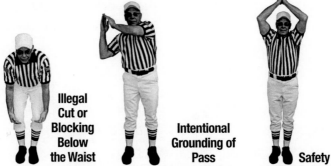

Illegal Cut or Blocking Below the Waist

Intentional Grounding of Pass

Safety

Years ago I was broadcasting a playoff game. The national radio broadcasters were in the next booth. When a critical kick was made I could hear the play-by-play man on the other side of the glass yell "Good!" I paused just long enough to see the official indicate that the kick was wide right. Never guess – even with extra points. Extra point kicks are almost always good! Kickers go years without missing one, but when they do it almost always affects the outcome. Don't call them automatically. Wait until the official's arms are raised and you will never be sorry.

Oops: My first association with the Eagles broadcast came as the host of the pre and post game shows. From there I moved into the broadcast booth as color analyst for a season. The play-by-play man at the time was a veteran announcer whose name was Charlie Swift. He was very intense, not a guy to make idle chatter off the air. But before that first broadcast he turned to me and said, "Kid, during a Sunday afternoon you say hundreds of things – some of them are going to be wrong!"

Members of the print media can reread their copy. They also have editors to catch mistakes before they go to press. Once something is out of our mouths, that's it.

In a career that has spanned three decades I don't think I have ever had a perfect broadcast. We're all human beings and human beings make mistakes. When players are tackled or even turned at a different angle their uniform numbers can become obscured. You'd be surprised at how easily an 87 can look like an 81 or a 28 can look like a 29.

Don't be afraid to correct a mistake. Early in my career I used to fear the possibility of misidentifying a player during a big moment. If it happens, simply correct the error and move on. It can happen to the most experienced broadcasters as well as the rookie.

Style: Don't concern yourself with developing a style. Just be yourself. Over the years your personality will come out during the broadcast. Don't force it. Don't invent catch phrases or signature calls. Stay away from clichés. Be clear, follow your fundamentals (remember STDD), and the rest will take care of itself.

Over time a certain phrase or inflection may add to the unique quality of your work, but let it happen – naturally. This applies to all sports.

THE GAME DAY CAST

Over the years the number of broadcasters involved in covering an event has changed. Originally one reporter handled the assignment. Then two people were dispensed to cover games. One handled the actual play-by-play and the second provided color commentary. Color commentary can take many forms – anywhere from background material about the participants to actual critical analysis of what's transpiring on the field. The emphasis on analysis opened the door for many former athletes to enter the broadcasting field.

When Monday Nite Football came to ABC television in 1970 they began with three men in the booth. Polished veteran Keith Jackson handled the play-by-play. Former Dallas Cowboys quarterback Don Meredith provided the color commentary and Howard Cosell created controversy, added humor and was either loved or hated by every football fan in America. "Humble Howard" and company turned NFL Football into an enormous spectacle. Cosell attracted the kind of attention that only a few icons like comedian Milton Berle commanded in the industry's early days.

In the years that followed "three man booths" became popular for many football telecasts. Some worked. Many didn't. Even some radio broadcasts added a third announcer with varying degrees of success. Often you had three people fighting for air time and at its worst they would talk over one another. It does work, however, in isolated cases. One is on Washington Redskins broadcasts when previously play-by-play man Frank Herzog and presently Larry Michael shares the booth with former Redskins' Hall of Famers Sam Huff and Sonny Jurgenson. Their broadcast has become a tradition with Redskins fans and the three men work well as a team.

Usually, however, a play-by-play man and color analyst can provide everything that the listeners or viewers need. The two men with whom I've worked the longest are former offensive lineman Stan Walters and former wide receiver Mike Quick. Stan was the analyst from 1984 through 1997 at which point he and his family moved to London, England where his wife, a high level corporate executive was assigned. Mike has been in the booth ever since. I've been fortunate to broadcast along side of two men who are both good friends and dedicated professionals. I've also worked closely with former All Pro middle linebacker Bill Bergey on many game day shows that have been both informative and fun largely due to our rapport.

Regardless of how well you know your color analyst it takes awhile to develop an on-the-air chemistry. When each man started I asked him to simply tap my knee when he wanted to come in with a comment. When he did I would immediately give him a nod. After awhile our exchanges became automatic and the tapping was no longer necessary. I could anticipate when each was ready with a pertinent comment and they could sense when I was looking for one. Each year in the booth the transitions become smoother.

The other thing a good color man understands is "word economy". He knows how to make an important point in the least amount of words so that the play-by-play man has time when the team breaks the huddle to describe the formation and pre snap motion.

The inexperienced color man might say –
"You're right Jim. What I saw there as I watched the play was the quarterback looking downfield and misreading the coverage. When that happened the linebacker had an easy interception."

The veteran color man making the same point would merely say –
"That was an easy interception for the linebacker. It occurred because the quarterback misread the coverage."

See, no extra words. Get right to the point and drive it home.

Here is another cardinal rule for a color analyst. Never speak while a play is taking place. There is nothing worse than hearing a big play described while the color man jumps in, yells enthusiastically and overrides the actual description. Save it. Wait until the play is concluded and then come on strongly. Two people speaking at the same time gives the listener nothing but noise.

SIDELINE REPORTERS

The sideline reporter is another job that was invented by television but has now been incorporated into many radio broadcasts.

My opinions may create some hard feelings but my objective is to be sincere and to tell you what I believe can contribute to the best possible broadcast. Many sideline reports are worthless! Adding an extra reporter increases the expense of the broadcast without increasing the revenue, unless they're separately sponsored.

A top notch sideline reporter is worth his or her weight in gold. Sideline reporters can add an entirely different dimension to the broadcast. The biggest problem is that too many reports appear to be prepared in the days leading up to the game. We do not need a sideline reporter to tell us a human interest story about a coach or player. We do not need a sideline report that tells us about something that occurred at Wednesday's practice. That can all come from the booth. The sideline report should focus only on something that is apparent from having that special perspective. That reporter can provide a close-up look and the first word on injuries. The reporter can hear the coaches and relay their concerns or reactions after a big play. Perhaps the official comes over to the sideline to clarify a call with the coach – the sideline person can report back and enlighten the audience about the ruling. Certainly the sideline reporter is in a much better position than the play-by-play man and color analyst to comment on the field conditions as the rain continues to pour or on the heat that the players are dealing with in an early season game. Former NFL defensive lineman Tony Siraguso is even able to use that perspective to comment on blocking schemes and other fine points that he observes from ground level.

Again – sideline reports can elevate a production if they have in-game substance but if they are simply another a way to say "See – we have a reporter on the sideline!", they are not only a waste of time – they're an unnecessary intrusion into the broadcast.

One time I would have given anything or paid any price to have a sideline reporter was on an unusually warm December 31st in 1988. Buddy Ryan's best Eagles team had captured the NFC East with a 10-6 record. The team practiced all week in Phoenix, Arizona and on Friday we flew to Chicago for the divisional playoff game against the Bears. This was a really special team with the enormously talented Randall Cunningham at quarterback and All Pros such as tight end Keith Jackson and wide receiver Mike Quick. The defense was one of the most feared in football featuring Reggie White, Jerome Brown, Clyde Simmons, Wes Hopkins, Byron Evans, Seth Joiner and Eric Allen. Expectations for this team were sky high.

Even after the Bears took an early lead I still felt confident that the Eagles would come back and win the game. Midway through the second quarter I noticed what I thought was a small cloud of smoke billowing up from the seats in the corner of the end zone. Color analyst Stan Walters said, "I think one of the fans has just lit a smoke bomb." Some smoke bomb! Within a matter of minutes the entire field was engulfed in fog. As we looked out of the broadcast booth we could see absolutely nothing! I mean nothing! I never thought it would last – but it did. I tried to keep things going with some attempts at humor. I remember saying, "I can tell that Randall Cunningham's having trouble – he's coming out of the huddle being led by a German Shepherd!" I tried every thing I could think of just to keep things going. It was beyond tough. I still thought it would clear up at any minute but in the third quarter nothing had changed.

The league sent the public address announcer down to the sidelines and at least he announced the down and distance and every so often he told us how much time remained. The Eagles lost but we managed to keep the broadcast from becoming a complete disaster.

If we had a sideline reporter or if we had been equipped with wireless microphones Stan and I would have gone down to field level and we would have actually been able to follow the action.

It was New Year's Eve day and I was convinced that we would never be able to fly home that night – that we'd be fogged in at the airport. Amazingly, minutes after the final gun, the fog dissipated and by the time we boarded the buses for the airport it was completely gone!

One of the things about this business is that you are never sure what you're going to see. Just when you're convinced that you've seen everything, something occurs which you couldn't imagine in your wildest dreams! That game is now known to millions of football fans as "The Fog Bowl".

INSTANT REPLAY

1. S.T.D.D. – Score – Time – Down – Distance – These basics are first and foremost.

2. Coordination with the spotter is essential for a smooth, accurate broadcast.

3. Your focus must be on the field at all times.

4. On close plays wait for the officials signals to determine first downs, touchdowns and field goals.

5. Sideline reports should only contain information derived from that special vantage spot.

BASEBALL

There's something very special about a summer night with the sound of a baseball broadcast in the background. When I flash back to memories of my childhood and teenage years there's always the sound of baseball accenting my reminiscence. Like millions of other kids, I enjoyed turning the dial on clear nights to see how many games I could pick up from stations around the country. It didn't matter if there was static or if the station faded in and out. For me, in Philadelphia, hearing Harry Carey and Jack Buck on a Cardinals game on KMOX in St. Louis or Bob Prince on KDKA in Pittsburgh was a complete triumph. What a thrill.

Meanwhile, the Phillies announcers beginning with Byrum Saam, Gene Kelly, and Bill Campbell came into our home every day or every night. I'd watch games on television but in those days only the away games and the home weekend games were on TV. Plus it was a lot easier to sneak a radio under my pillow and listen into the wee hours of the morning when the Phils were playing on the west coast. Especially on school nights.

The baseball broadcaster becomes a greater part of your life than the broadcasters of any other sport. In the first place they do over 180 games a year between March and October. Secondly, there's something about the pace of a game that allows their personalities to come through to a greater extent. The best broadcasters have an innate ability to communicate on a very personal level. They seem to be speaking only to you.

Ever since Harold Arlin broadcast a Phillies – Pirates game from Forbes Field in Pittsburgh on KDKA on August 5, 1921 great personalities have emerged from the airing of "America's Pastime".

While hitting the jackpot and attaining the lofty perch of the major leagues is difficult to attain – there are probably more opportunities to develop than in any other sport. For one thing, there are hundreds of minor league teams throughout the country. They offer a young broadcaster a wonderful opportunity to hone his skills. The best thing about baseball is the number of games. I am a staunch believer in relentless practice. Doing games day after day really allows a young announcer to reach a comfort level with his audience.

The other plus is that most minor league teams are affiliated with major league franchises. You'd be amazed at how many people have moved up from the minors. Sometimes the parent club has an opening and they elevate a broadcaster who is getting rave reviews at their triple A affiliate. Once you're in baseball you become aware of what openings are occurring and you have an opportunity to take a shot.

When I was a teenager the Phillies used to have a contest each year that was sponsored by The Atlantic Refining Company. They invited young listeners to write a letter in 200 words or less telling why they wanted to be a sportscaster. They even called it the Junior Sportscaster Contest. Five or six finalists were chosen and invited to Connie Mack Stadium for a game where they were given the chance to tape record one inning. A winner was chosen and that person actually got to broadcast an inning along with the Phillies regular announcers. Each year I submitted my 200 words. Each day I rushed home from school hoping against hope that I'd be chosen as a finalist. It never happened.

One of the people who won the contest was a teenager from the Harrisburg, Pennsylvania area by the name of Andy Musser.

Years later after graduating from Syracuse University, serving in the armed forces and holding a succession of radio and television jobs, Andy actually ended up as a Phillies broadcaster. He remained as part of their broadcast crew for about twenty five years.

After about four or five years of frustration I finally sat down and wrote a letter to Gene Kelly. I told him about my great desire to one day be a sportscaster and asked him for advice. For weeks I heard nothing. When I had all but given up I received a letter post marked St. Louis, Missouri. During the visit for a Phillies – Cardinals series Gene Kelly actually answered my correspondence. I couldn't believe it. My heart pounded as I carefully opened the envelope hoping to avoid so much as nicking the words of wisdom inside. After reading it I carried it around for weeks and to this day the now yellowed stationary is in safe keeping. The one phrase that still stands out was a quote from the legendary Dodgers' President Branch Rickey who supposedly said "Luck is the residue of hard work."

You must have luck on your side to end up in any of the top Major League or NFL or NBA or NHL jobs. Only the truly fortunate can become successful sports talk hosts on major market stations or big time television sports anchors or network hosts. But the truth is these jobs do exist. To be in position to compete you have to put in the work, tons of it! You've heard the saying that it's who you know – not what you know. It has only a grain of truth. The longer you hang in there – the harder you work – the more people you get to know –the more contacts you are able to make. Eventually one of them may pay off.

Whether it's baseball or any other sport, you need that luck but if you aren't prepared all of the luck in the world and all of the contacts won't help you attain lasting success.

7/11/58

MR. MERRILL ALLEN REESE
7614 WOODBINE AVE.
PHILADELPHIA 31, PA.

DEAR MERRILL:

THE ONLY ADVICE I CAN OFFER REGARDING BECOMING A PLAY-BY-
PLAY SPORTS ANNOUNCER IS TO PREPARE YOURSELF PROPERLY
THROUGH PROPER COURSE OF STUDY, EXPERIENCE AND BACKGROUND
SO THAT WHEN YOUR BREAK COMES ALONG, YOU'RE READY FOR IT.

I THINK BRANCH RICKEY, SR., PUT IT APTLY WHEN HE SAID THAT,
"LUCK IS THE RESIDUE OF HARD WORK". SOUNDS SIMPLE BUT IT
ISN'T.

IF YOU HAVE SUCH A CAREER IN MIND, MIGHT I SUGGEST A GENERAL
LIBERAL ARTS COURSE AT A SCHOOL THAT FEATURES JOURNALISM,
SPEECH AND DRAMA, WITH A GOOD ATHLETIC PROGRAM, BOTH VARSITY
AND INTRAMURALS. I CITE THE LATTER BECAUSE THIS GIVES YOU
AN OPPORTUNITY TO STUDY PLAYS AND PLAYERS AT A COMMON LEVEL
AND IN THOSE SPORTS, YOU YOURSELF ARE ABLE TO PARTICPATE IN.
AS WELL, OFFICIATING INTRAMURAL SPORTS IN A SCOOL OF THIS
TYPE GIVES YOU FIRST-HAND EXPERIENCE THAT YOU CANNOT BUY.

IN OTHER WORDS, CHOOSE A SCHOOL WHERE YOU CAN COMBINE WORK
AND EXTRA-CURRICULARACTIVITY TO PREPARE YOU FOR THE LONG
HAUL AND THAT PROVIDES A WIDE SCOPE OF OPPORTUNITIES AT
MEETING PEOPLE AND SEEING THEM PERFORM UNDER PRESSURE.

THERE IS NO GUARANTEED KEY TO THE SUCCESS OF ANYONE. I
WOULD SAY MAKING FRIENDS, AND ABOVE ALL, KEEPING THEM IS
THE BEST WAY TO ACHIEVE SUCCESS, FIRST AS AN IDIVIDUAL,
SECOND AS A CAREERIST. MANY THANKS FOR YOUR INTEREST.

SINCERELY, RESPECTFULLY

GENE KELLY

Letter from Gene Kelly - circa 1958

SCORING

Every baseball broadcaster keeps score. There are easily obtained scorebooks available for this purpose. While everybody develops their own individual method, there are certain basics that are followed. Every position has a number for scoring purposes. This has nothing to do with the uniform numbers. They are:

1. Pitcher
2. Catcher
3. First baseman
4. Second baseman
5. Third baseman
6. Shortstop
7. Leftfielder
8. Centerfielder
9. Rightfielder

In some scorebooks, each box contains a small diamond so that the scorer can indicate whether the hit was a single, double, triple or home run. It is easy to keep track of the base runners on the diamond. Using the numbers the scorer can quickly see how an out was made. For example 6-3 would indicate that the batter grounded the ball to the shortstop who threw to first to retire the batter. A small loop with a 7 would tell us that the batter flied out to left field. E-4 would tell us that the batter reached first due to an error by the second baseman.

The letter K indicates a strike out. A backwards K indicates that the batter took a called 3rd strike. Again – everybody has their own individual method of scoring. It's important that this is done neatly and accurately so that the broadcaster can easily recall everything that took place in the course of a game! Everyone develops their own method of scoring a game.

Keeping score is something that many fans do at home while watching a telecast or listening to a broadcast. For the prospective baseball broadcaster it's a good thing to do as often as possible so that it becomes almost automatic.

Atlanta

Umpires:

Avg.	HR	RBI	Visitor (0-0)	Pos.	1	2	3	4	5	6	7	8	9	10	11	12	AB	R	H	RBI
			Diaz	9	L-6		1-3		5-3			HP								
			Prado	4	H-R		K		1-B			1-B								
			C Jones	5	W		K		13			1-B DP								
			McCann	2	F-9			F-8		4-3		6-5								
			Anderson	7	W			F-5		W K DP		4-3								
			Escobar	6	FC			W		4-3 DP		F-9								
			La Roche	3		F-4		1-B			K	F-8								
			Gorecki	8		5-3		K			L-6									
			Norton	PH									K							
			Jurgens	1		5-3			K		K									
			Totals		R		0	0	0	0	0	0	0							

No.	Pitchers	W-L	IP	H	R	ER	BB	SO	HR	WP	HB	DP			SH	
												2B			SF	
												3B			LOB	
												HR			E	
												SB			PB	
												CS				

EXTRAS
Bench   Bullpen

Avg.	HR	RBI	PHILLIES (0-0)	Pos.	1	2	3	4	5	6	7	8	9	10	11	12	AB	R	H	RBI
			Rollins	6	F-7		F-8		4-3		F-9									
			Victorino	8	F-8			1-3		F-9	F-7									
			Utly	4	F-8			H-P		G-3	F-6									
			Howard	3		F-8		F-8		F-8		K								
			Werth	9		K		4-3		FC	2-B									
			Ibanez	7		5-3			W		W	W								
			Feliz	5			F-8		1-B		E-5	K								
			Ruiz	3			2-B		1-B GDP		2-B									
			Blanton	1			4-3		L-3 DP											
			Stairs / Madson	PH / 1							K									
			Eyre / Lidge	1																
			Totals		R		0	0	0	1	0	2	0							

No.	Pitchers	W-L	IP	H	R	ER	BB	SO	HR	WP	HB	DP			SH	
												2B			SF	
												3B			LOB	

Page from scorebook

Harry Kalas

PLAY-BY-PLAY

In Philadelphia and throughout the Delaware Valley no broadcaster had a greater impact than Harry Kalas. The magnificent voice of the Phillies joined the club when they opened Veterans Stadium in 1971 and remained their announcer until his death on April 13, 2009 at the age of 73. I first met Harry when I was a young radio reporter and he was introduced to the local media by the Phillies for the first time. Several times in those early years I'd ask him for advice when I saw him at various events. He was always approachable and willing to sit down and offer words of encouragement.

One of the real bonuses of writing this book was the opportunity it provided me to spend time with outstanding broadcasters. Never did I realize when I met with Harry on a snowy afternoon, February 3rd, that it would be the last time our paths would cross. We spoke about his Hall of Fame career. He was inducted at Cooperstown, New York in 2002 into baseball's broadcasters' wing.

Harry reminisced that day about growing up in Naperville, Illinois and listening to baseball on the radio. He spent his first year of college at Cornell College in Mount Vernon, Iowa. In that freshman year his speech professor, a blind man named Dr. Walter Stromer told him that his voice was perfect for a career in broadcasting.

After graduating from The University of Iowa in 1959 Harry was drafted into the Army. He was assigned to the 27th Infantry and sent to Hawaii. His unit needed a broadcast specialist and he was chosen for the job.

Near the end of his tour a job opened with the minor league Hawaii Islanders and again Harry was at the right place at the right time. After four seasons with the Pacific Coast League triple A team he was ready for the next step. That occurred in Houston where he was hired as the Colt 45's became the Astros and moved to the first major league domed stadium – the Astrodome. The rest is history. We spoke about the many aspects of his job and how he went about calling a game.

Rather than using a scorebook Harry kept track of the game on score sheets. After the game he recorded all of the vital information into a book which he brought with him to every game. The notes he saved included every pitcher who worked, who hit homeruns, who had RBI's and all of the other pertinent statistics from that game. While he acknowledged that preparation is vital for success, the preparation for a baseball broadcast is quite different than what a broadcaster experiences in football. In the first place there's a game almost every day. Also teams generally meet for at least 3 games in a row. In football there are teams you see only once a season. There's also a buildup in football that takes place all week with elaborate game plans formulated and implemented. In baseball, scouting is more extensive than ever but it's still pitcher versus hitter.

Often writers and broadcasters congregate near the cage when teams take batting practice. It was during BP where Kalas discovered his signature homerun call, *"I was standing around the batting cage in the mid 70's . Greg Luzinski hit one way off into the upper deck in left centerfield at Veterans Stadium. Larry Bowa was looking at it and said 'Wow! That's way outta here.' I heard that and I thought that's got kind of a neat ring to it. So that's how I started "Outta here." I have Larry Bowa and the Bull to thank for it."*

The key is to let things happen naturally. Spending time inventing phrases or calls is a mistake. These moments will either come to you or in the case of Harry Kalas just hit you when you're not looking.

The baseball broadcaster calls every pitch from the time the pitcher looks down at the catcher. He describes the pitcher's wind up (or stretch) and his delivery. He also identifies the kind of pitch – whether it's a fast ball, curve, slider, knuckler, change-up, etc. He should also give listeners a picture of how the fielders are positioned – whether the leftfielder is playing close to the line or whether the infielders are up – looking for the bunt or the shift is on for the lefthanded hitter. Remember – this is all about painting a picture.

Never anticipate an umpire's call. Wait until you see him indicate whether a pitch is a ball or a strike, or whether the ball hit down the line is fair or foul.

Following fly balls and gauging their distance takes a lot of practice. After a while you're able to tell by the sound the bat makes at contact ("the crack of the bat") just how well the ball was hit. You can also see how the outfielders are moving. They've developed instincts that enable them to react instantly. There's an old comedy routine about the inept broadcaster who yells *"There's a long fly ball to deep left field – it might go – uh – the shortstop backs up and makes the catch."* This won't happen to the experienced broadcaster although wind in different stadiums (especially Wrigley Field in Chicago) can carry a routine fly ball into the seats for a homer or turn a really well hit ball into an easy out. The pace of a baseball game is different from any other sport. There are no clocks to determine when an inning begins or when a game ends. While there are certainly intense and dramatic moments, there are also slow stretches where nothing spectacular occurs. That's when the play-by-play broadcaster and the color analyst can keep listeners interested with lively conversation. If a game is one sided and noncompetitive it is not unusual for the broadcasters to chat about something unrelated to the game situation. That's fine except – you still must refocus for every pitch.

Example:

"Hamels goes into his wind up, kicks, comes to the plate – high ball one. Next week the Phils begin their West Coast road swing. We're looking forward to seeing the Dodgers for the first time this season. Strike – Hamels with the fast ball. He nipped the outside corner of the plate. The count stands at 1 and 2."

Harry Kalas worked with many other broadcasters over the years – most notably the late Richie Ashburn (one of the most popular former athletes in the history of Philadelphia), likeable former Phillies pitcher Larry Andersen and Chris Wheeler, a broadcaster who is a tremendous student of the game. Harry marveled at legendary Dodgers' broadcaster Vin Scully. Scully has been broadcasting Dodgers games since 1950 and he remains masterful behind the microphone. Scully does not work with a color analyst. He does the games by himself, however, he has such vast knowledge and a deep reservoir of experiences that he is able to handle it effortlessly. He weaves stories in and out yet at the same time the listener never misses a pitch or is left wondering about what just happened.

The late Red Barber used to say that he used a 90 second egg timer to tell him when to repeat the score. It's frustrating for a listener to wait until the end of an inning to find out who's winning. Assume that most listeners tune in and out and require constant updating.

Example:

"Two outs here in the bottom of the fourth. The Phils lead 3-0 on Ryan Howard's two run shot in the first and Jimmy Rollins RBI single in the 3rd."

There's one situation in baseball where there are varying opinions – how to handle a no-hitter. Harry Kalas broadcast quite a few no hitters and did not believe that it was his job to respect the superstition of not referring to that feat while it's still in progress. Kalas said, *"I've always wanted the listener to know that something special is happening. It may not happen but I still want people to know that this guy is pitching a no hit, no run game – here in the 7th, still a no-hitter."* The broadcaster is there to chronicle the game – to describe it – to transmit the feeling that those at the stadium are experiencing. Nothing he does will affect the outcome. It is his job to make certain that his audience is aware of everything that's transpiring – especially with something as rare an accomplishment as a no-hitter.

SILENCE IS GOLDEN

Even on radio, don't ever feel the need to fill every space between pitches with words. The baseball broadcast has a rhythm all of its own. Kalas remembered being paired with Richie Ashburn for the first time and Ashburn saying, *"Harry, if I don't have anything pertinent to say, I won't say anything."* That was fine because when Ashburn did have something to say it was either the kind of information baseball fans devour or it was something humorous that added to the enjoyment of the game.

A few uninterrupted seconds of crowd noise – not cheering but that sustained murmur from time to time actually adds to the unique quality of the baseball broadcast.

INSTANT REPLAY

1. Baseball broadcasters keep an easily deciphered score sheet as they're describing the game.

2. Develop the ability to gauge the distance of fly balls by watching the reactions of the fielders and hearing the crack of the bat.

3. All conversation between broadcasters must be spaced around the description of every pitch.

4. Constantly update the score and innings. Assume listeners may have tuned in late.

5. Don't over talk. The sound of the spectators between pitches is welcomed from time to time.

BASKETBALL

Marc Zumoff and Ed Pinckney

As a student at Temple University, the first sport I really had a chance to immerse myself in as a broadcaster was basketball. I used to drag my heavy Webcor tape recorder up three flights of steps, unroll the extension cord and plug it in at rickety old South Hall. I sat in the balcony, way out of listening range and practiced play-by-play while the basketball team scrimmaged for legendary coach Harry Litwack.

Finally I got the opportunity to display what I had learned on WRTI-FM, the student run radio station. As a sophomore, junior and senior, I described every game played at the University of Pennsylvania's Palestra. The Palestra was home for all of the "Big 5" teams – not just Penn. That meant that Temple, St. Joseph's, LaSalle, and Villanova played almost all of their home games there. It was not unusual for me to describe doubleheaders on Wednesday, Friday, and Saturday nights.

One Saturday afternoon the Philadelphia Public League had three high school playoff games on that court. After describing those, I quickly downed a couple of hot dogs and saddled up again to do a college doubleheader – that meant that I did five games that day. Know what? I would have done ten! The more the merrier! Regardless of the sport – a young broadcaster should seize every opportunity. You learn something from each broadcast. You may not hear that improvement from game to game, but it is occurring – especially if you're diligent about your work. I suggest listening to a recording of your play-by-play when you have a spare hour or two and jot down notes on a pad. You can also ask a player, coach or communications professor to critique that tape. There are things that we say or do that we don't recognize – we need others to point them out. Take the criticism in the right frame of mind.

Evaluate what others say. There are some things that you will agree with but there are other suggestions that don't make sense. Put them through a filter. Don't accept everything at face value. I happen to love golf. It's nice to receive a tip from time to time while at the driving range but if I listen to too many people I'll end up totally out of sync. It's the same with broadcasting. There are certain unalterable fundamentals that apply but in terms of approach and style there are a lot of variations.

One person who understands this and is widely recognized as one of the nation's top basketball broadcasters is Marc Zumoff, the television voice of the Philadelphia 76ers. In 2010 Marc began his 17th season in the NBA.

As a young boy he was smitten with the broadcasting bug and began to imitate disc jockeys by doing introductions to the records on his phonograph.   He also loved sports so he graduated to watching television, lowering the audio, and announcing play-by-play into his tape recorder.

Zumoff also went the college route as a communications major at Temple University. His early professional background consisted of a wide range of assignments including television soccer. He found his true nitch when he started doing halftime interviews on 76ers basketball.

Like all of us, Marc has tremendous passion for his sport. *"I love it."* He says, *"I get to watch the greatest athletes in the world."*

Zumoff's spread sheet sample

JOHN KUESTER — ASST W/L. BROWN ('76)
AND WIDE? 2004 (TITLE)
ALSO 76 ASST 05-06
1ST TIME HEAD NBA...
AFTER 14 YRS ASST NBA
HEAD COACH COLLEGE...
BOS UNIV & G. WASH...
PLAYED COLLEGE D. SMITH
3 YRS NBA 70'S AFTER...
3RD RD PICK KC KINGS

DARRELL WALKER
BRIAN HILL
PAT SULLIVAN
HAT: MIKE ABDENOUR

CLOSE GAMES
2-1 (3+)
100
AFTER 3
(+) 9:3; (-) 1:19 (0-7 H)

SEASON
GOTTEN R. HAMILTON & T. PRINCE BACK (INJ)...
BUT HASN'T HELPED; [S] 11X. (LONGEST) 1993-94
LAST W 12/12 V GS (H); OFF SINCE WED L @SA
SKED? LAST 10 GPS: 7 ON RD & 1 OF 3 (H) GPS V. LAL
LAST: 8 SEED; ELIM. 1ST RD PIO'S AFTER 39 WINS
FIRST TIME FINISHED BELOW .500 IN 8 YRS
THAT ENDED STREAK 50 W SEASONS AT 7
ALSO BROKE STRETCH 4X CENTRAL DIV TITLES
HAD W DIV 6-PREV-7 YRS; IRONICALLY ONLY YR...
(STRETCH?) DID NOT W DIV 2004 (IND) & W TITLE!

OT
0-1 (11/21) @UT

IF DETROIT WINS
BREAK [S] L X11; 1ST W SINCE 12/12 (GS)
12-23 ON [S]; TAKE SS FR 76 WITH ONE TO PLAY
76: 3RD X L AFTER 3-2 (WEST TRIP)
JUST 6 PLAYERS LEFT FROM LAST YR
GONE: R. WALLACE, A. IVERSON, A. MC DYESS...
A. AFFLALO, W. HERRMANN JUST NAME FEW
AMONG 14 PLAYERS: 3 ROOKIES

SKED
SOME STRUGGLES...
ATTRIBUTABLE TOUGH SKED...
MIDST STRETCH 9 OF 14 RD...
INC. 2 TRIPS (TEXAS)
MON @CHI; TUE @WAS

TEAM		
PTS	91.5	>96
REB	-2	
FG	44%	47%
FT	72%	
3P	28%	34%
T/O	>14	>14
BL	<4	
ST	<7	

---

3 RODNEY STUCKEY 6-5 205 E. WASH
27P DET W (WACH) DEC. INC. SHOT V. IGUODOLA...
AFTER ANDRE BLOCKED INITIAL ATTEMPT
LAST INCR FR 5PPG TO 13PPG
15TH PICK 2007 DRAFT
2 YRS AGO: SURGERY ON LEFT HAND
EASTERN WASH BIG SKY CONF
LEFT COLLEGE AFTER SOPH YR;
AVG <29PPG & <24PPG 2 YRS COLLEGE
<19 4A 1.5S 42 83 (7-36)19
5 2A 17M 35 94 (9-39)23

17 CHUCKY ATKINS 5-11 185 S. FLA
SIGNED FA; 35 YRS OLD;
2ND TIME W/DET; 1ST TIME AROUND TRADED...
MIDDLE 2003-04 [S] R. WALLACE (NO RING)
IN ALL 8 NBA; SPLIT LAST YR (OKC & DEN)....
IN FACT HELPED BEAT 76 LAST YR @DEN
OTHER TEAMS: ORL, BOS, LAL, WAS & MEM
ORLANDO NATIVE; MAYNARD EVAN HS (DDT)
CROATIA; CBA; NEVER DRAFTED
4 4 14M 53 41 (1-0)

38 KWAME BROWN 6-11 270 HS
WELL IN 2ND DET WIN HERE DECEMBER
1ST EVER (HS) #1 PICK NBA DRAFT (M. JORDAN)
28 ON 3/10
TRADE TO LAL THEN TO MEM (P. GASOL) DEAL
NOT WELCOME ANYMORE WASH # ISSUES
SUSP BY WASH (PIO'S) 4 YRS AGO
GLYNN ACADEMY BRUNSWICK GA; 25 IN MARCH
ORIG BORN CHARLESTON (SC)
11 8 12 4A 27M 43 76.5 (7-32)22

---

32 RICHARD HAMILTON 6-7 195 UCONN
OUT 26 OF 34 GPS: SPR [R] ANKLE AND (HAMSTRING)
3X (AS); LED DET SCORING LAST 7 XYRS; 32 ON 2/14
COATESVILLE; 8TH YR DET; 7TH (H) (H) PTS >10K [C]
3PT% TITLE 4 YEARS AGO
WEARS MASK BECAUSE RE-INJ NOSE (SERIOUS)
#7 PICK; NCAA TITLE AS JR.
MOST OUTSTANDING FINAL 4 (27 V. DUKE)
40 11A 1.5S 42 83
31 9A <19 40 76.5 (7-31)23

7 BEN GORDON 6-3 200 UCONN
STARTER FOR R. HAMILTON (INJ)
W/C. VILLANUEVA 2 KEY FA SIGNEES
[C] <21PPG LAST W/CHI (MOMENTS PIO'S V. BOS)
[C. 41.5%, 3PT; ROOKIE [S]; 6TH/YR AND #2 ROOK/YR...
(E. OKAFOR) (T-MATE) UCONN; #8 PICK 2004...
LEFT UCONN AFTER JR YR & NCAA (W/C. VILLANUEVA)
BORN LONDON ENG MOVED SHORTLY AFTER BIRTH...
36 16A MT. VERNON NY (HS)
13 9A <18 33M 44 83 (33-100)33

12 WILL BYNUM 6-0 185 GA TECH
BEEN HOBBLED (L) ANKLE SPRAIN
TOUGH SCORER OFF BENCH
W GAME HERE V 76 LAST YR (GREAT 4TH QTR)
2 YRS AGO; BACK NBA (2 YRS) EUR & ISRAEL
HANDFUL GP (05-06); SAME YR #1 NBDL PPG
UNDRAFTED AFTER 4 YRS COLLEGE BALL
2 YRS GA TECH AFTER TRANSFERRED FR ARIZONA
30 19 CHICAGO NATIVE;
11 8 12 4A 27M 43 76.5 (7-32)22
4 3.5 13M 54 53 (0-0)

---

6 BEN WALLACE 6-9 240 VA UNION
14 RPG 1ST 2 GPS V. 76
FA; 35; 2ND TIME W/(DET); PREV STINT 6 YRS
4X DEF/YR & 4X (AS); TITLE 2004
[C] 6.5, 10.5, >2B; [C] 6, 10, 2B; #1 (F) (H) BLKS
1ST UNDRAFTED (NBAH) START (AS)
PREV 1 1/2 YR W/CLE AFTER 1 1/2 YRS CHI
HUGE FA SIGNING BY CHI 2006; BULLS TRADE TO CLE
ALSO ORL & 3 YRS (WAS) (PAID PART $$ CAMP)
1 OF 6 (NBAH) #1 REB & BLKS (S); KAJ...
<4 <10 1B 29.5M 46 47 (0-0)
51 29 14

9 CHRIS WILCOX 6-10 235 MD
FA SIGNEE; 20 OF 34 GPS BEF TONITE
BOTH STARTER & BENCH PLAYER NBA [C]
GOOD POST-UP
COUPLE YRS W/SEATTLE 13PPG STARTER
DET 5TH NBA; LAST YR OKC & NY; ALSO LAC
#8 PICK OFF ROSTER NCAA CHAMP TEAM
W/JUAN DIXON & STEVE BLAKE (NCAA) U OF MD
AVG 12 & 7 (MID) FINAL (S) (SOPH)
22 28 10B
11 18 3B
48 30

---

22 TAYSHAUN PRINCE 6-9 215 KENTUCKY
OUT 26 OF 34 GPS W/DISC PROB ENDING STRK 497X GPS
W/R/P & B. WALLACE ONLY 2004 TITLE TEAM
4X MEMBER NBA 2ND TEAM ALL-DEF
COMING OUT PARTY (V. 76) 2003 PIO'S
#23: ALL 4 YRS V. KENTUCKY
DRAFT AFTER JR (S) (W/DREW); 17.5PPG (SR)
GEO. YARDLEY AWARD BEST (HS) S. CHANDLER
DOMINGUEZ HS (COMPTON) TYSON CHANDLER
<10 4 39M 43 56 (2-10)

5 AUSTIN DAYE 6-11 200 GONZAGA
GOTTEN MINS IN 31 OF 1ST 34 GPS (S)
GOT SOME SKILLS; LONG ARMS
FATHER DARREN DAYE; 5 YRS W/WAS, CHI & BOS
15TH PICK LAST SUMMERS DRAFT
LEFT GONZAGA AFTER SOPH YR (AVG 13 & 7)
PRETTY GOOD SHOTBLOCKER AS WELL
4.5 2 13M 45 60 (13-41)32
13 7 14 5 27M 44 60 (39-127)31

35 DAJUAN SUMMERS 6-8 240 G-TWN
2ND PICK (1 OF 2 ROSTER) (J. JEREBKO)
LEFT SCHOOL AFTER JR YR
AVG 14 & LAST YR; 28TH G-TWN (H) SCORING
LOOKING FOR 1ST NBA POINTS
JUST 1 GP BEF TODAY; JUST 1M
32 24
12 9

---

54 JASON MAXIELL 6-7 260 CINN
[C] 6 & 5 GUY LTD ACTION MOSTLY OFF BENCH
PLAYS FOR THE CONTACT
26TH OF 30 PICKED 1ST RD 2005 DRAFT
YOUR BASIC UNDERSIZED PF
AVG 15 & <8 (SR); GREAT BLOX COLLEGE
AVG 3 BPG SR
CARROLLTON, TEXAS
34 10
14 7 5 4 18M 46.5 61 (0-0)

31 CHARLIE VILLANUEVA 6-11 230 UCONN
BROKEN NOSE EARLIER (S)
W/B. GORDON 2 KEY FA SIGNEES; 3RD NBA
LAST 3 YRS W/MIL (WHO ACQ TRADE) FR TOR
BORN QUEENS NY BUT FAMILY FR DOMINCAN REP.
ALOPECIA AREATA: AUTOIMMUNE DISEASE...
RESULTS LOSS HAIR SCALP OTHER PARTS BODY
MET GOOD # KIDS SAME DISEASE; "LIFE ALTERING...
NOT LIFE THREATENING"
28 15
13 9

33 JONAS JEREBKO 6-10 230 SWEDEN
CHANCE START EARLIER (S) (INJURIES)
2ND RD; BLUE COLLAR; 10 & [T] (C)111 R W (WAS)
NATIVE OF SWEDEN
PLAYED PRO BALL IN ITALY LAST YR
BEF THAT 2 YRS SWEDEN'S PRO LEAGUE
FATHER PLAYED COLLEGE SYR & PRO BALL EUR
ALSO MEMBER SWEDISH NAT'L TEAM
3 1 9M 31.5 75 (8-19)42
22 11

TEAM

PTS	102	
REB	-5	
FG	45%	48%
FT	78%	42%
3P	34%	
T/O	14.5	15.5
BL	<6	
ST	8.5	

IF 76ERS WIN
BREAK 2XL;
4TH W LAST 5 RD GPS
DET: [S] 12TH X L 4TH LONGEST DET (F) (H)

SKED
MON N.O. 7P (CSN)
WED NY 7P (CSN)
FRI SAC 7P (CSN)
MON (MLK) @MIN 330P (CSN)
THEN 2XH
WED 1/20 POR; FRI 1/22 DAL
CSNPHILLY.COM
WATCH GPS H-DEF: DVR CAPABILITY

V. DETROIT
3RD OF FOUR
1-1: L LAC (12/19) 112-107
W @NY 10/31 (141-127)
PISTONS W 1ST 2 GPS...
76 L BY 4 (WACH) DEC...
21 LEAD CHANGES...
3 GP HOMESTAND
DET W HERE NOV BY 7...
76 NOW HOPE RD CONTINUES (KIND)...
THEME: 76 OUTREB AVG...
12.5RPG 1ST 2 GPS; DET...
AVG 18.5 OBS

AT&T; 749377

SEASON
L LAST (WACH) TOR 108-106
76 WHOPPING 9 GPS DECIDED BY 3 FEWER
ONCE AGAIN FAILED HOLD DIF LEDE 2ND HALF
76 FAILED GET LINE 4TH QTR
NEARLY 1/2 LOSSES BY 6 OR FEWER
76 W 3-LAST-4 RD ALL COMING...
DURING RECENT 5 GP (WEST) (3-2)...
W @DEN, @SAC & @POR
76 RD WIN % BETTER THAN (H) WIN %

EDDIE JORDAN   MIKE O'KOREN (ASSOC)
ANOTHER CLOSE LOSS...   RANDY AYERS
LAST NITE FOR 76 DROPPING...   JIMMY LYNAM
108-106 GP TO TOR (WACH)   AARON MCKIE
WASH D.C. NATIVE   HAT: KEVIN JOHNSON
5+ YRS WAS (P/OS 4X)
4 YRS LEAD ASST'NJ NETS...   AFTER 3
FINALS 2002 & 03   100
1 1/14 (S) HEAD SAC KINGS (90'S)   DEF (+) 4-17; (-) 6-8
PLAYED NBA 70'S & 80'S
RUTGERS (FINAL 4) 76   CLOSE GAMES
                               4-5 (3<)

---

3 ALLEN IVERSON 6-0 180 G-TWN
NWT (L)KNEE); DENIED CHANCE FORMER TEAM
[S] 22P LAST; ALL 4 ASST (1ST) QTR
901ST GP OF HALFTIME [C] TONITE [C] (#3) (F) (H)...
LAST 900TH GP OF HALFFAME [C] (#3) (F) (H)...
GAMES PLAYED: #1 H. GREER, #2 D. SCHAYES
10+ [S] (76); 2ND (F) (H) PTS (H. GREER) >19K PTS
[C] <27PP #6 (NBAH) #2 (ACTIVE) LEBRON
OUT 4 GPS (L) KNEE ARTH
DEN TRADE TO DET (C. BILLUPS)
(76) ACQ A. MILLER & J. SMITH; 34
(3 GPS) MEM (FA) AFTER HAMSTRING (PRE) [S]
#1 (76) (H) 3PTA & 3PTM
NO ONE PHILA [C] MVP THAT YR
76 FINALS 2001; MVP THAT YR
4X [C] PPG TITLE; 2X (AS) MVP; 9X(AS)
ONLY (NBAH) #1 NBA STLS 3X(S) (SINCE 73-74)
(NBA) STLS P/G GP (10) V. ORL 5/1399
ONLY (C) T/O (WACH) 1/7/02 V. LAC; 30P 10R, 11A
<15 >A 31M 47 81 (4-9)

23 LOU WILLIAMS 6-1 175 HS
23P (3-9PTM) LAST; EXAMPLE WAY PLAYED LATELY
28 FT HEAVE FINAL POSSESSION LAST NITE NE
BROKEN JAW (11/24 @WAS) (A. JAMISON) (26P)
OUT LESS THAN 1/2 ORIG 8 WKS (12 GPS)
SOUTH GWINNETT HS (SNELLVILLE) (GA) (112-HR) ATL
MID 2ND RD; 1ST (76) (HS) D. DAWKINS (#5) '75
#1 HS PLAYER USA: 23 (10/27)
>16 >A 1.5S 49 83.5 (30-94)/32

33 WILLIE GREEN 6-3 200 DET MERCY
DETROIT NATIVE RELISHES PLAYING (PALACE)...
FAIR SAY: PER MIN PRODUCTION BETTER STARTER
8 PREV STARTS: >16PPG, 50% FG
[S] 26P 12/5 @CHA (20P 3RD QTR)
TRAINER: PERSPECTIVE LIFE AND B-BALL
(L) KNEE SURG AUG '05; GREAT BOUNCE BACK [S] LAST YR
NEWLY-RENOVATED L-ROOM NAMED FOR ($$)
2ND RD SEA; DRAFT NITE; B&B DETROIT
22 7A 8.5 21M 44 85 (17-57)/33

11 JRUE HOLIDAY 6-3 R 180 UCLA
1ST V.S. DET [S]; DNP-CD HERE NOV, (SHLD INJ DEC.)
AARON: MORE LEGS INTO HIS SHOT
ALMOST AS MANY THINGS LEFT HANDED AS RIGHT-HANDED
17TH PICK 2009 DRAFT; 19, YOUNGEST NBA
ONLY YR (BRUINS) OUT POSITION (2-GUARD)
8.5PPG 45% FG ONE YR UCLA (BEN HOWLAND)
#1 HS PT GUARD USA CAMPBELL HS...
CHATSWORTH, CA (L.A AREA)
>5 2.5A 18M 36 76 (15-49)/31

---

1 SAMUEL DALEMBERT 6-11 250 SETON HALL
2XDO/S; 10 & 10R LAST; [S] 26P & [S] 2OR TUE...
V. WASH; LAST (T0R) FOLLOW UP L/U LATE PUT...
76 UP BEF C. BOSH QUESTIONABLE GOOD & FL
17 & 11 76 (L) WACH (DET) DEC.
308T HXGP (#3 ACTIVE-A. MILLER, D. FISHER)
20% RAW; REST ORGANIC; BUILDS OWN LAPTOPS
HAITI; MONTREAL TEEN (CANADIAN NAT'L TEAM)
#27 2001; 34 GP ROOKIE; NEVER 3PTM
8A (0-0)
31 7A <7 8.5 >2B 25M 49 84 (0-0)

14 JASON SMITH 7-0 240 COL. ST.
DNP-CD LAST; LTD MINS TUE (WASH) AFTER...
AFTER WELL AT DEN SUN...
7P (8M) LATE 3RD-EARLY 4TH @DEN (INC. 3PTM)...
MISSED ALL LAST YR TORN ACL (L) KNEE (AUG 2008)
SOLID ROOKIE [S]; MISSED JUST 6 GP (MOST) INJ
KERSEY COLORADO (POP. 1500); AGR. COMM...
60 MILES NE OF DENVER; YOUNGEST 4 KIDS
20TH PICK MIA; ACQ DRAFT NITE TRADE
>3 2 >11M 41 68 (9-23)/39

25 RODNEY CARNEY 6-7 205 MEM
BEEN MYSTERY MAN IN TERMS (76) ROTATION...
SHOWED DURING TRIP CAN BE GP CHANGER...
THEN JUST 3M V. TOR LAST NITE
FA; DNG-GO-ROUND W/76 AFTER YR W/JEZ) & MIN
AFTER 2 YRS (76) TO MIN (CAP ROOM) (E. BRAND)
#16 OH; SWAP PIX; CONF USA PLAYYR
#1 MEM (H) [C] 3PTM; BORN MEM; HS (INDY)
ALL 4 YRS MEM
6 2A >4M 41 82 (20-54)/37

---

9 ANDRE IGUODALA 6-6 205 ARIZONA
IN SPITE 76 STRUGGLES CONTINUES EXCEL...
LAST: -1A 5TH [C] T/O -17P, [T] [S]11R, 9A, 3S...
47 MINS IN FRONT END OF B-1-B
AND HE DEFENDS AND NOT JUST (STEALS)
[S] PTS & REB (32 & 11) @NY 10/31
LAST: W/LEBRON; C. PAUL & D. WADE...
ONLY AVG 18, 5R, 5A; LED NBA MINS PLAYED
LAST: ALL 82 GP 4TH X IN 5 YR [C]; AVG 38MPG [C]
2 YRS ARL; 1ST LOTT L. HUGHES (8) '98
18.5 <7 <6A <2S 40M 43 76 (45-143)/31.5

16 MAREESE SPEIGHTS 6-10 245 FLA
8 GPS AGO; [C] 28P, 9R V. LAC 12/19...
SINCE THEN HAD MAKE MOST LTD P/T
19P, 23M HERE NOV THEN KNOCK KNEES W. BYNUM...
NOT AS EFFECTIVE AFTER; THAT INJ NOT RELATED...
(L) KNEE SPR 11/14 @CHI; MISSED 14 GPS
#16 (SOPH); 2ND OF 2 NCAA TITLE TEAMS
ST. PETERSBURG FLA (HS); PREP SCHOOL VA...
9R 4B
14 7 28 FB OB; QUIT CONCENTRATE B-BALL
<12 >5 2M 54 78 (0-0)

72 JASON KAPONO 6-8 215 UCLA
DNP-CD LAST AND 3-PREV-4
REPETITION AND CONSISTENCY MORE THAN FORM
[S] 20P @BOS 11/25
FR TOR JUNE (R. EVANS); #1 NBA 3PTM% 2007 & 08
[C] >45% (3PT) [T] S. KERR #1 3PT% (NBAH)
[C]; TOR, CHA & CLE; OFF BENCH MOST [C]
FINISHED #3 (UCLA) (H) PTS (D. MACLEAN, KAJ)
14 >5 >14M 43 (4-9) (30-74)/40.5

---

21 THADDEUS YOUNG 6-8 220 GA TECH
19P; (3R LAST; 18P BUT (9-24 FG).
2-L AST-19 (3PT)
NOT SHOT WELL PREV 2 GPS V. DET
12/14 V. GS; [S] 26P; [C] 14R
LAST 1/4 OF [S] AVG >21PPG, >56% FG
20 LAST 6/21; 12TH PICK AFTER 1 YR GA TECH
FATHER FELTON YOUNG 8TH RD PICK BUFF BRAVES (LAC)
HONORS STUDENT (HS); 4.3 GPA; #21 (FAN POLL)
BORN N.O.; MOVED MEM 4TH GRADE
31P
<15 >5 45 66 (28-83)/34

42 ELTON BRAND 6-8 255 DUKE
DNP LAST (WACH) STOMACH VIRUS
BRAND REDUCED MINS V. WAS TUE AFTER...
TERRIFIC MINS @POR & @DEN
[C] 20, 10R 3A, 2B, >50%FG, 74% FT; 31 ON 3/11
LAST FEB: SURG TORN (R) LABRUM (29 GP)...
RUPTURED (L) ACH. TENDON DURING WIO (8/07)...
#1 CHI '99; CO-ROOKYR (S. FRANCIS); 2 YRS CHI
LEFT AFTER SOPH; 1 OF 4 DUKE (1ST RD); NAT'L PLAYER/YR
PEEKSKILL NY; DUKE FINALS HIS LAST (S)
28 10
<14 7 >1B 30M 49 78 (0-0)

7 PRIMOZ BREZEC 7-1 255 SLOVENIA
FA; 5 GPS; INACTIVE PREV 5; 3RD NBA; C (18, 4R, 19MPG
LAST; ITALY 3 YRS CHA (EXPAN DRAFT)...
LATE 1ST RD IND; RARELY PLAYED 1ST 3 YRS
SLOVENIA 4TH EUR C-SHIPS (SUMMER); TURKEY 2010
STARTED WITH SLOVENIAN NAT'L TEAM @15
SPEAKS ITL, SLOV, ENG & YUGO
20
2 4 9M

Preparation is something that never stops. *"I have an obligation, to stay on top of everything that happens in the NBA all year long – read every publication, stay in constant contact with the latest happenings, even during the off season."*

The game day preparation is also intense but it doesn't involve as much uniform number memorization as football and hockey. *"The reason,"* Marc explains, *"is because we're generally right there on the floor, courtside. We know what every player looks like plus we see teams multiple times. Identification is not a problem in the NBA for either the radio or the television play-by-play man. College and high school broadcasts are different. Many of the players are not familiar and that's when thorough uniform number memorization becomes a must."*

For each game Marc goes on the internet to obtain information and transcribes much of it onto spread sheets which are accessible during the telecast. Into each player's block he writes key statistical information as well as personal interest items. You can never be too prepared. There are games that flow with constant action that are competitive and dramatic throughout but there are others that are one sided or are not examples of the sport at its finest. *"We also see games,"* Marc says, *"That lack continuity – that start and stop and seemingly contain an endless succession of fouls – that's when all of that information that I've compiled pays off."*

Marc also attends game day "shoot arounds" where he gets a good idea of how the players are feeling and also experiences a preview of what their strategy might be for the upcoming game.

PLAY BY PLAY

It's not a broadcaster's job to make a game exciting. We can't do that. Fans are far too knowledgeable. They know what they're watching. But it is our job to keep the broadcast interesting – packed with pertinent information and thought provoking comments.

Marc Zumoff feels that the most difficult part of basketball play-by-play is dealing with the tempo changes in a game. You can anticipate one kind of game and get the complete opposite but you have to be prepared for the unexpected. *"Think of a story line going into the game but prepare to shift gears if it doesn't materialize."* It could be that your team has been winning games with red hot outside shooting. That's what you anticipate. But on this night they can't hit the side of a barn. Then the story focuses on their ability to find another way to compensate. Perhaps you call on your memory bank.

Example:

"Tonight they're really off the mark but earlier this month they were cold from the floor but went inside to do most of their damage. Let's see if that works tonight."

In football I talked about my S.T.D.D. (Score, Time, Down Distance). Minus the down and distance, the score and time must always be available for the basketball listener. On radio the score must be given after every basket - foul shot or field goal. For the telecaster that isn't always the case because the score constantly appears on the screen. Instead, Marc will deal with trends such as, *"Holiday's 15 footer gives the Sixers a ten point lead. He's scored 8 of their last ten points!"*

The telecaster can also point out other things while a team is setting up a play. For radio you have to stay much more basic. You describe most passes but not all. If the guards pass the ball back and forth three or four times you can cut out a pass or two and then follow the ball as they send it inside to the low post or into the corner. You should never miss the pass that sets up a shot.

It's the same with rebounds on radio. Sometimes it's impossible to mention everyone who gets a piece of the ball. A fitting description might be:

Example:

"There's a real battle for the rebound and finally Smith comes down with the ball." Then as they're moving down court you might add, "Smith went way up and took that rebound away from Jones."

Don't try to say too much in too short a time frame or the listener will receive a muddled picture. Look for various ways to describe things – don't become too predictable. Keep your broadcast fresh. As a player comes across mid court don't always say that he brings it across the 'mid court stripe'. You can also call it 'the ten second line'. A player doesn't always move across 'the paint'. It can also be referred to as the 'foul lane' or simply 'the lane'. Variety is the spice of an interesting broadcast.

We all have pet phrases – in every sport – but try not to work them to death. I've been identified with a long, extended, inflection rising, *"It's gooooood!"* after a game changing Eagles field goal, but, I rarely use that for a 30 yarder early in the game.

It's the same in every sport. Marc's voice reflects the impact that a play has on the game. It doesn't have to occur only in the last few minutes. He says, *"There are times when we see a great play – it could be midway through the third quarter yet you have the feeling that this play is pivotal to the game's outcome. You want to show that with your inflection."*

In an NBA game there's a danger of inferring too much too early. We've all seen 16 point leads evaporate as quickly as a puddle on a summer day. Save those memorable calls for the truly special moments.

Zumoff even takes it further than that. *"While each game counts the same in the standings, there's no doubt that the wins and losses become more critical as you head down the stretch late in the season. With the playoffs in sight, there's so much more on the line. Your broadcast should reflect this – the whole tone of your broadcast or telecast transmits the sense of importance of these games."* They really are special and all of us in each of our sports lives for these big games!

The college and high school teams play shorter seasons, much shorter, so each individual game has a sense of importance. Also, schools have special rivalry games which are really a lot of fun to be a part of. Almost every broadcaster cuts his eye teeth on high school and college sports.

The higher the level, the more acceptable it is for the broadcaster to be critical. I'm not talking about what is referred to as a 'hatchet job'. Ripping teams and players apart is never acceptable for a professional behind the microphone. Unless, of course, we're talking about something out of the ordinary like a blatant personal foul or an action intended to injure an opponent.

Good, solid, appropriate criticism is not only acceptable but adds to a broadcast. On the college level and especially on the high school level it makes sense to be a little less severe with our critiques.

OFFICIALS

Basketball officials have to be in excellent shape to keep up with the action. Like officials in every sport they're human and do make mistakes. Pointing out mistakes is fine but Marc Zumoff has a personal rule, *"If I want to criticize an official for a mistake I'll do it only if I haven't seen a video replay. It's unfair to be critical if I've seen a replay in slow motion and he made his call in real time. That doesn't mean that I can't point out a mistake after a replay, but, I might add that it was a very difficult call to make. I am just as quick to praise an official for getting a tough call right."*

In the NBA the video replays used by officials work really well. They use them at the end of quarters to tell if a shot was taken before time expired. They can also use it to determine whether a field goal was taken from 3 point range or whether the player stepped on the arc and the shot counts for 2 points. For this they will rarely stop the action. The adjustment is made during a time out at the end of the period and the changes, if necessary, are made on the scoreboard.

Scoring

Because of the amount of scoring, statistics are a big part of a basketball broadcast. For an NBA game both the telecaster and the radio play-by-play announcer are provided with a monitor which exhibits a running box score. A look at the screen reveals point totals, rebounds, assists and most everything else the broadcaster needs. Still – many employ an additional statistician to keep track of scoring runs and other information that will add to the game.

For college or high school a statistician is needed. Basketball is too fast for the play-by-play person to keep score. A few may, but, not many. If the broadcast is done on a tight budget – the engineer can keep score and pass individual point totals over to the play-by-play announcer on small pieces of paper.

It is so important for the broadcaster to be aware of the personal and team fouls. That's why they must be kept either electronically or by somebody on the crew.

Many times for high school broadcasts you're able to find a student or a parent more than willing to help out. Bring a scorebook. Set it up to your liking and clearly explain what you want them to keep. You can also devise a few simple hand signals for the statistician to use before giving you information.

Example:

A 'T' in this case could mean 'team fouls' not a 'technical foul' or 'time out' if used by officials.

It doesn't matter which signs you devise as long as you and your stat guy or color analyst are on the same page. Teamwork by the broadcast crew is just as important to the success of your production as it is to the success of the team on the court.

RAPPORT

Many broadcasters travel with their teams. Flying by charter is a lot more convenient these days than flying commercially. In the first place, you don't have to worry about making your connection in another airport. Second, it gives the players an opportunity to get to know you. That's a lot more important than many might think – not just from the ego standpoint. Establishing rapport with players and coaches is a key to getting inside information. While much of this information might not be 'airable', at least it gives you a background which contributes to your understanding of what the team is experiencing.

While most colleges have sports information departments few high schools do. Having a pleasant working relationship with the coaches can contribute so much to the job you do on the air.

In the absence of news releases and media guides, some personal insights from the coaches can put your broadcast on another level.

It's also a good idea to attend practices from time to time and when the opportunity presents itself engage the players in conversations. Find out interesting facts about their backgrounds, their other interests, their favorite athletes, and their dreams and aspirations. Even in a fast paced sport like basketball you'd be amazed at how many opportunities you'll have to work human interest elements into the broadcast.

Just learning the numbers and describing the action doesn't cut it. Regardless of which successful broadcaster I approach, regardless of their sport, the first thing they stress is always the same – P R E P A R A T I O N !!!!

Occasionally you'll learn something that is not for public consumption. You may hear players criticizing a coach, or an assistant coach might let some personal information slip. File it away, but don't ruin valuable relationships by revealing privileged information that could lead to trouble.

PARTNERS

Marc Zumoff has always had good chemistry with his color analyst and it shows. For Marc this is very important. *"I want the audience to feel that we're two friends, hanging out and watching basketball with them. What could be better? I look for ways to set up the analyst. I might lead to him with some information that we both share. I might say that so and so is having a great night off the boards – and he'll say 'Yes, he's got 14 rebounds already!' Or if I know he uncovered some really interesting information before the game, I'll find a way to lead him into it."*

Again, these are the things that make a broadcast special. Marc likens the job of the telecaster to that of a master of ceremonies. *"I'm referring to what the camera shows – I'm bringing in the analyst – I'm going to the side line reporter – recapping earlier action – listening to the director in my earpiece and leading in to a commercial break. There is so much going on – I feel like the ringmaster! It's really an exhilarating experience."*

ONE MORE TIP

Try to stay just a beat behind the action. Sometimes you're screened from seeing who took the shot from the corner or who actually deflected the shot. Don't jump to conclusions – take that extra second and be sure.

Even on radio it's helpful to let the sound tell the story. When that crucial foul shot swishes through, allow the roar of the crowd to say "It's good!" before confirming the obvious and updating the score.

INSTANT REPLAY

1. The score must be given after every basket.

2. Individual point totals and rebounds along with personal and team fouls must be updated as the game continues.

3. Don't describe every meaningless pass. Slow down the action to paint a more easily visualized picture.

4. Allow the drama to build. Don't show too much emotion too early.

ICE HOCKEY

Jim Jackson

No sport presents a greater challenge for the broadcaster than ice hockey and nobody handles it more skillfully than the Philadelphia Flyers' voice Jim Jackson.

Like most of us, Jim got his initial experience on the student station in college. By his sophomore year at Syracuse University he was developing his play-by-play talents describing football, basketball and lacrosse. After graduation Jim was hired by his hometown radio station in Utica, New York. When his station got the rights to broadcast the Devils of the American Hockey League he got a great opportunity. Growing up, Jim had attended a lot of minor league hockey games and loved the sport. The American Hockey League was the equivalent of triple A in baseball – one step from the major leagues.   After six years and exactly 499 games Jim sent tapes to every club in the National Hockey League. He got positive responses from both the Flyers and the Anaheim Mighty Ducks. After working out a contract with the Flyers, Jim became their radio play-by-play man for two years before moving to television. There he replaced hall of famer Gene Hart who had been with the team since its inception. In 2010 Jim began his 17th season with the club.

Jim feels that the only way to learn hockey is to experience it in person. Radio and television can capture excitement but there's no substitute for actually being at the games. He points out, *"You can listen to some of the great hockey announcers like Mike Emrick, the late Gene Hart, Gary Thorne, or Dan Kelly and enjoy it but I really think you fall in love with hockey in person."*

PREPARATION

Jim Jackson believes in extensive preparation for every game. He used to watch Gene Hart carrying a big black book filled with notes to every broadcast. People wondered where he'd find the time to use so much information. Unlike football where there's time between every play or baseball where the very nature of the game provides room for stories, hockey action is practically non-stop and when the players do stop skating it's time for a commercial. Jackson remembers Hart saying that he only uses about ten percent of the information he compiled but, *"I never know which ten percent I'm gong to need."*

Jim prepares two very detailed roster sheets with all of the players' vital information and statistics. He keeps a notes column on the right hand side containing the player's draft information and any kind of personal interest story. He points out, *"I don't know how often I actually refer to those sheets, but from putting the information in, a lot sticks in my memory."*

Jim memorizes the uniform number of each player on the roster. Hockey's a change-on-the-fly sport where there's rarely a chance to look down. You know who the goalies are so it's necessary to memorize 21 skaters. Three won't play so you basically have to be able to instantly identify 12 forwards and 6 defensemen on each team. This isn't easy. It takes a lot of work. Even for football I walk around with flashcards all week. For hockey the memory work is constant. As tough as this may be, it seems to get a little easier the more you do it.

Jackson really focuses on the players during the skate before the game. They go through some drills where you can check your ability to identify them quickly. Since he knows the

Flyers inside and out he needs only to focus on the opposition. Their pre game skate gives him about 15 minutes of valuable preparation.   He will also put the line combinations (left wing, center, right wing) on his sheet in a block on the right so that he can quickly refresh his memory at a glance.

PHILADELPHIA FLYERS
23-19-3 (have won 4 straight; 8-1-1 in last 10)
ON ROAD: 11-10-1 (5-1-1 in last 7)

NO	PLAYER	G	A	P	NOTES
COACH	PETER LAVIOLETTE- 1st yr w/Pha; 8th, 45				10-8-2 2nd us-born wins 2nd Adams;Cup '06 US Oly hc '06 2 yrs NYI hc (ahl)-Calder,coach of yr '99 11-yr pro def
3	OSKARS BARTULIS- D RK;22 6-2,196 Ogre, Latvia	0	6	6	2g, 13pts, 4/80gp w/ahl Pht '09 1g, 21pts/57gp w/Phant '08 13g, 48pts/55gp w/Cape Bret. (qmjhl) '07 31 nhlgp 3rd yr pro 3rd pick Pha '05 3 yrs qmjhl Top Def B-Pool World Jr's 12/06 31gp.-13 (*t2nd lwst rks) 1x mt pt Latvian olyp 2g, 4pts/12gp w/ahl Ad "methodical;good composure"
5	BRAYDON COBURN- D 3RD;24 6-5,220 Calgary, AB	5	9	14	7g, 28pts, +7/80gp '09 Car. high 9g, 36pts '08 led Pha w/+17 led Pha def goals '08 2yr ext 11/07 4th yr w/Pha; Atl vet acq for Zhitnik 3g-4a/20gp w/Pha;0g-4a/29gp w/Atl '07 1st pick (8th) Atl '03 Ank inj-missed 1gm 2x mt pt 1x 2 goals whl all-star
11	BLAIR BETTS- C 6TH;29 6-3,210 Edmonton, AB	6	3	9	Fa signee-1yr deal 10/09 6g, 10pts/81gp w/NYR '09; co-"player's player award" 2g, 7pts w/NYR '08 NYR, Cgy vet *28 goals/345 nhlgp 3x shldr surg 2nd pick Cgy '98 "energizer, but sometimes brittle" 26gp Dislocated shdr-missed 19gms total ppg 2x 2 goals Flyers 18-6-2 when he plays
12	SIMON GAGNE- LW 10TH;29 6-0,195 Ste Foy, Que	6	12	18	34g, 74pts, +21, 12ppg, 4shg/79gp '09 7g, 18pts/25gp '08;missed 57gms w/conc 5yr deal '06 627 nhlgp, all w/Pha car.high 4 47g, 79pts '06 7x 20 goals; 4x 30; 2x 40 2x all-star 2x Can Olyp-Gold '02 5gm pt strk (1g-5a) 5g-8a/12gp since ret 21gp Abd surg-24gms 3x mt pt 1st pick Pha (22nd) '98
13	DAN CARCILLO- LW 3RD;24 6-0,205 King City, Ont	4	6	10	3g, 14pts w/Pho, Pha '09; 1st nhl w/254pts; 4th w/22 fights acq for Upshall, 2nd pick '11 3/09 2nd yr w/Pha;Pho vet 2yr deal 7/08 13g, 24pts/57gp '08; led nhl w/ 324pm echl vet 3rd pick Pit '03 Susp-4gms 1 goal/last 13gp 116pm (2nd) 10 fights 1x 2 goals;1x mt pt 2x 29+ gls ohl
14	IAN LAPERRIERE- C 16TH;35 6-1,200 Montreal, Que	3	9	12	fa signee Pha 7/09 7g, 19pts/74gp w/Col;led Col w/163pm led Col pm/last 3yrs;led LA pm 2x Col; LA(9 yrs), SL, NYR vet car. high 21g, 45pts w/Col '06 12x 100pm 140pts qmjhl '93 7th pick SL '92 2g-3a/last 5gp 13 fights 2nd act w/190 fights, 4th pm
17	JEFF CARTER- C 5TH;25 6-3,200 London, Ont	16	22	38	Car. high 46g, 84pts '09; 2nd nhl gols, 4th shts;1st Pha g, pts, +23, 13ppg, 12gwg (1st); all-star 3yr deal 6/08 352 nhlgp, all w/Pha 29g, 53pts '08 3x 20 goals t7th rks v 23 goals '06 1st ahl w/po g, pts '05;Calder 4g-7a/last 9gp *3rd nhl shots 259 cons gp 5x 2gls;11x mt pt 1st pick Pha (11th) '03
18	MIKE RICHARDS- C 5TH;24 5-11,195 Kenora, Ont	19	20	39	Car. high 30g, 80pts, +22, 8ppg '09;1st nhl w/7shg;Selke nom 28g, 47a, 75pts '08;All-Star;5 shg (13th nhl) 335 nhlgp, all w/Pha 2x 20 goals;once 30 10g, 32pts '07;missed 23gms, shldr. hern. Calder Cup '05 2 fights Can olymp capt can'05 wrld jr's-gld 1st rd pick Pha (24th) '03 4yrs w/Ktcr;MemCup'03 5gm pt strk (3g-3a);6g-6a/last 10gp 9ppg (*t3rd) shg 1 ht 4x 2 gls;8x mt pts
19	SCOTT HARTNELL- LW 9TH;27 6-2,210 Regina, Sask	11	16	27	Car. high 30g, 60pts, +13, 143pm/82gp '09;1st nhl w/54 mnrs 24g, 43pts, 159pm/80gp '08 6 yr deal-7/07 3rd yr w/Pha; 1st 6 yrs w/Nash acq w/Timonen for 1st pick '07 6/07 4x 20 goals;once 30 3 conc Goal/last 2gp after 17 straight w/o one 6ppg 5x mt pt 3 fights 1st nhl w/29 minors 1st pick Nash (6th) '00
20	CHRIS PRONGER-D 16TH;35 6-6,214 Dryden, Ont	6	26	32	acq w/Dingle for Lupul, Sbisa, 2 1st picks 6/09 11g, 48pts/82gp w/Ana '09 susp 8gms-stomped Kesler '08 5th team Ana, Edm, SL (9yrs), Hfd vet 13g, 59pts w/Ana '07;Cup; t6th def pts *6x all-star Hart, Norris '00 5gm pt strk (1g-7a) *7th def pts 7x mt pt 4x 50pts 8x 10+gls 4x Can Olyp-gld '02 1st pick Hfd (2nd) '93
21	JAMES VAN RIEMSDYK-LW RK;20 6-3,205 Middletown, NJ	10	17	27	1g, 2pts/11gp w/Pht '09; 17g, 40pts/36gm at U of New Hamp 11g, 34pts/31gp w/U of New Hamp '08 39 nhlgp, all w/Pha head inj-2gms; flu-1gm 1st pick Pha (2nd) '07 2x US Wrld Jr 3g-4a/last 5gp;3g/last 4gp 5gwg (*t4th) *t4th rk pts, t2nd assts, t4th gls 1x 2gls;7x mt pts nhl rk of Nov
25	MATT CARLE- D 4TH;25 6-0,205 Anchorage, AK	3	21	24	5g, 26pts/76gp w/TB, Pha '09; 4g, 24pts/64gp w/Pha '09; acq w/3rd pick for Eminger, Downie, 4th pick 11/08 2nd yr w/Pha; TB, SJ vet 2g, 15pts/62gp w/SJ '08 11g, 42pts '07;1st nhl rk def pts;all-rk 2nd pick SJ '01 1g-4a/last 3gp is +18 5x mt pts u of Den prod;2x chmp;hby bkr'06

Jackson's Game Notes

#	Player				Notes
26	**DANNY SYVRET - D** 3RD ;24 5-11, 203 Millgrove, Ont	2	2	4	No pts/2gp '09; 12g, 57pts/76gp w/Pht;2nd ahl def pts acq for Potulny 6/08 2g, 20pts w/ahl Spr, Her '08 / 2nd yr w/Pha; Edm vet 1g-3a/44nhlgp 0g-1a/16gp w/Edm '07 3rd pick Edm '05 23g, 69pts/62gp ohl '05 / u. body inj Scratched 9x overall 21gp 2g, 8pts/11gp w/ahl Adr
27	**MIKA PYORALA-LW** 1ST ;28 5-11, 169 Oulu, Fin	2	2	4	fa signee Pha 7/09 21g, 43pts/55gp w/Timra (sel) '09 17g, 33pts/46gp w/Timra (sel) '08 / 35 nhlgp, all w/Pha 7 yrs in Fin ('01-'07); 28 goals/56gp '07 / Scratched last 8gms; 10 of last 11 9 straight w/o pt 1 goal/last 17gp
28	**CLAUDE GIROUX- RW** 2ND ;22 5-11, 172 Hearst, Ont	10	18	28	9g, 27pts, +10/42gp '09; 17g, 34pts/33gp w/Pht no pts, 2gp w/Pha '08 Gold Can World Jr's '08 / 89 nhlgp, all w/Pha 38g, 106pts w/qmjhl Gat '08;2nd pts; po mvp 1g-1a/5gp w/Pht '07 / Goal/last 2gp -8/last 5gp 1 fight 6x mt pt 2x 2gls 1st pick (22nd) Pha '06
32	**RILEY COTE- LW** 3RD ;27 6-2, 220 Winnipeg, Man	0	0	0	0g, 3pts 63gp '09;5th nhl w/174pm, (4th w/22 fights 1g, 4pts, 202pm/70gp '08;2nd nhl w/24 fights '08; 4th pm / 153 nhlgp, all w/Pha 3 yr deal 7/08 no pts/8gp w/ Flyers '07 parts of 3 yrs w/Phtm 4x 200pm min. / 12gp scratched last 9gms;32x 3 fights 97 straight w/o goal 1 goal/153 nhlgp undrafted
36	**DARRELL POWE- C** 2ND ;24 5-11, 212 Saskatoon, Sask	8	3	11	6g, 11pts, -8/60gp '09; ps goal; 4g, 7pts/8gp w/ahl 9g, 23pts, 133pm/76gp w/ahl Pht '08 / 89 nhlgp, all w/Pha 2g, 4pts/11gp w/Phtm '07;13g, 28pts/34gp w/Prctn ahl fa signee '07 Prctn prod / 2g-3a/last 5gp Career high goals; tied pts 2x mt pt Shldr inj-missed 16gms
44	**KIMMO TIMONEN- D** 11TH ;34 5-11, 194 Kuopio, Fin	4	20	24	3g, 43pts, +19/77gp '09; led Pha def pts, Ashbee 8g, 44pts '08;led Pha def pts; Ashbee 6 yr deal / 3rd yr w/Pha; Nash (1st 8 yrs) vet 3x all-star 2x Ashbee 40+pts/7 straight yrs led team def pts/8 yrs / 1g-3a/last 5gp 4x mt pt 1x 2gls 11th pick LA '93 3x Fin Olyp-Slvr '06
45	**ARRON ASHAM- RW** 10TH ;31 5-11, 205 Portage la Prairie, Man	4	9	13	8g, 20pts, 14 fights, car. high 155pm/78gp '09 fa signee Pha 7/08-mlt yr 6g, 10pts/77gp w/NJ '08 / 2nd yr w/Pha; NJ, NYI, Mtl vet car. high 15g, 34pts w/NYI '03 3rd pick Mtl '96 2x 40 goals, 90 pts whl / 1g-5a/last 5gp 38gp 2x mt pts 6 fights oblique inj-4gms Scratched 1st 3 gms
48	**DANNY BRIERE- C** 10TH ;32 5-10, 179 Gatineau, Que	16	15	31	11g, 25pts/29gp '09; groin, abd inj-missed 53 gms 31g, 72pts/79gp '08;5th nhl w/37pp pts; team low -22 / 3rd yr w/Pha; Buf, Pho vet fa signee 7/07-8yrs car. high 32g, 95pts '07 5x 20 goals, 3x 30 1st pick Pho '96 / 2g-5a/last 4gp 5gls/last 9gp susp 2gms quad inj-4gms 5x 2gls; 9x mt pt 1 fight
29	**RAY EMERY- G** 4TH ;27 6-2, 196 Cayuga, Ont	11-8-1	2.83	.901	fa signee Pha 6/09 22-8-0, 2.12, .926/36gp in Russia '09 12-13-4, 3.13, .890/31gp w/Ott '08 / 1st 6yrs pro w/Ott org 33-16-6, 2.47 '07 9-0, 1st 9nhlgp, rec 4th pick Ott '99 Can mj jr goalie of yr '02 / vs. Tor: abd surg-missed 18gms 0-4/last 5 starts; .806 sv%
33	**BRIAN BOUCHER- G** 10TH ;33 6-2, 200 Woonsocket, RI	4-11-1	2.84	.896	Fa signee Pha 7/09 12-6-3, 2.18, .917/22gp w/SJ '09 3-1-1, 1.76, 1so/5gp w/Clb '08;23-16-1, 2.47 w/Pht / 3rd stint w/Pha org SJ, Clb, Chi, Cgy, Pho vet nhl rec 5 cons SO's w/Pho '04 1st 5 yrs pro w/Flyers' org / vs. Tor: fing inj last start: 12/21 1st nhl ga '00,4th sv%; all-rk 1st pick Pha '95
49	**MICHAEL LEIGHTON- G** 6TH ;28 6-3, 192 Petrolia, Ont	9-4-1	2	.8	Waiver claim 12/09 6-7-2, 2.92/17gp '09 2yr deal 6/08 1-1-0, 2.66/3gp w/Car '08;28-25-4, 2.10 w/ahl Alb / 2nd stint w/Pha; Car,Nash, Chi vet 4gp w/Pha '04 25-35-13/86 nhlgp 3 yrs ohl 6th pick Chi '99 / vs. Tor: *8-0-1, 2.13, .928-11gp w/Pha started 10 straight 4th nhl ga, sv% in Dec

PP	42 for 174 % ( )	8 for 17-last 4gp; 12/32, 37.5%-last 10gp 6 SHGA (*27th)
PK	159 of 197 % ( )	killed 21 straight; 35 of 37-last 10gp 4 SHG
RT	HITS: Carcillo 103, Laperriere 85, Powe 79 BLOCKS: Pronger 108, Timonen 92, Carle 70 CHANCES: Carter 162, Richards 109, Hartnell 84	
	TOI: Pronger 26:08, Richards 20:15 FO%: Carter 51.4%, Betts 51.1%, Richards 50.6%, Giroux 48.9%, Powe 47.8%	

INJURED: RYAN PARENT (BACK), OK TOLLEFSEN (KNEE)
-LEAD NHL WITH 234 MINOR PENALTIES, 1ST WITH 61 STICK PENALTIES; 2ND WITH 41 FIGHTING MAJORS
-FLYERS ARE 1-13-0 WHEN TRAILING AFTER TWO PERIODS; 2ND WORST IN NHL

12	18	28
19	17	48
21	36	45
13	11	14

25	20
44	26
5	3

GAME TIME

Years ago few players wore helmets so you could quickly identify them by just knowing what they looked like. Today that isn't possible. Jackson focuses on the numbers that players wear on their sleeves. You're calling the game from somewhere close to mid ice and you can't depend on the player to turn so that you can get a full view of his chest or back. The sleeve numbers are smaller but they are still readable and almost always in view. The broadcasters are usually seated at the highest point in the building but the play-by-play man will rarely use binoculars. The analyst will, however, from time to time.

Because of the speed of the game and the broadcaster's vantage point it is sometimes difficult to be certain who scored the goal and who will be credited with an assist. Fortunately, immediately after scoring most players make it clear that the goal came off their stick. Sometimes goals come off of a deflection. The experienced announcer will just bide his time until he is certain. The announcer never wants to get a break away goal wrong. That can be embarrassing. Jackson recalls, *"I remember one game at Madison Square Garden where we're a long way back and Scotty Hartnell, who had two goals, took a long pass at center ice and I couldn't tell if the number was 18 or 19 – Mike Richards or Hartnell, so I tried to stall while showing excitement, but I wasn't completely sure until he scored, spun and showed me his number. You never want to misidentify a player who is completing a hat trick!"*

It's the same in football – don't guess! It's better to wait an extra few seconds rather than call a big play and have to make a correction.

The only time when following the puck can be a problem is on a deflection but regardless of speed the black puck stands out against the white ice.

74

The hockey announcer must constantly give the score and the period. This is something you simply can't overdo, especially on radio. On television you can see it on the screen. Because hockey is so free flowing you can very easily get caught up in the play but you must remember that the listener may have tuned in at any time. Wondering about the score is extremely frustrating.

The hockey announcer follows the puck describing where it's located, who's in control, the movement of the goalie and the physical contact and checking that takes place. When there is a crunching check against the boards he strives to make the listener feel the impact. At the same time, the broadcaster attempts to slow the game down a bit so that the listeners can develop a clear mental image of what is taking place. A machine gun delivery with words coming out a mile a minute will leave listeners confused. By slowing the game down I don't mean lagging behind the action. Simply eliminate meaningless passes. Jackson explains, *"If a defenseman has the puck in his own zone and he's passing it across to his defensemate there's no need to talk about that. It's not going to lead to anything that has any effect on the game. Any pass that potentially can effect the game should be called, especially passes around the goal, but if you call every pass it will only cloud the picture you're attempting to paint."* The passes between defensemen deep in their own zone may provide the perfect opportunity for the broadcasters to recap the score and other bits of information.

On obvious goals the broadcaster can be very authoritative but on those that can be borderline it is best to watch the official for the ruling. The hockey goal has the red light to indicate a score but Jim Jackson doesn't always trust it. He feels that the red light isn't always reliable. Hockey is so fast that there's a natural tendency with even the best and most experienced announcers to jump the gun. Be careful. There are a lot of shots that go in and come back out so quickly that they almost look as if they had hit the post. There are many instances where goals must be reviewed by the officials at the league offices. As in football they must have clear cut, indisputable evidence that the original call was incorrect. If the replay is inconclusive the original ruling stands.

When the replay is on the monitor both the radio and television broadcaster will refer to it and interpret exactly what they are seeing.

The only time that the hockey broadcaster uses his monitor is to describe a replay. Even if he is far from the action he must still focus on the ice. Hockey is a game in which the puck is practically a blur and all too often the monitor will not allow you to anticipate and follow the direction.

NOBODY'S PERFECT

A slip of the tongue, a misidentification, a botched call of a goal are mistakes that can occur on any hockey broadcast. The broadcaster, however, can't harp on them. Nobody likes to make mistakes but the error-free broadcaster has yet to be born. The great athletes have short memories. A missed foul shot doesn't mean that a string of misses will follow. In fact, the great shooters keep firing believing that they're only a jump shot away from going on a hot streak.

In hockey the best goalies believe that they can stop any shot. If they let one in, they consider it an aberration. The same with the broadcaster. You can't dwell on a mistake – correct it and move on. Sometimes you can even make a lighthearted remark, making fun of yourself. Do not let it affect your confidence.

Sometimes things slip out of our mouths that we don't hear. We don't realize that we used a wrong name. People do this all the time in normal conversation but on the air we think it's a big deal. Jackson remembers, *"The Flyers were playing the Ottawa Senators and they have a young player named Nick Foligno. His father is Mike Foligno who played for the Buffalo Sabres. Well, without even knowing it, I'm calling Nick, Mike Foligno his first shift on the ice. The next time I called him Mike the director said in my headset "It's Nick". Right on the air I corrected myself and said, "Did I call him Mike? It's Nick Foligno and he does play a lot like his dad."* That was a perfect way to correct a mistake.

Years ago I would slip from time to time without realizing it and refer to Dallas running back Emmit Smith as Emmit Thomas who was the Eagles defensive coordinator. My color analyst at the time was former Eagles' offensive lineman Stan Walters and when either one of us did it we'd owe the other guy a dollar!

IN THIS CORNER

Like it or not fighting is prevalent in hockey. It's hardly uncommon to see players remove their gloves and go at it toe to toe – or in this case skate to skate. At that point the hockey broadcaster merely shifts into the mode of a fight announcer and describes blow by blow. Jim Jackson actually enjoys that role from time to time as long as nobody gets seriously hurt. His job is to put the listener in the arena and tell him everything that happens. Says Jackson, *"I want them to see that fight. I want them to know that guy got his jersey pulled up or that guy's getting rid of his elbow pads."* It's a side show, of course, but it can be very entertaining for the hockey fans. It has always been a part of hockey and it's not going away.

OFFICIALS

Ice hockey is one of the most difficult sports to officiate. While officials in all sports have to be in decent physical condition, none move as quickly as those in hockey who have to be expert skaters. They also must have great eyes in order to follow the puck. They need the strength necessary to break up the aforementioned fights.

The hockey officials also have to expect to get more than their share of loudly voiced criticism from the home fans. While it's natural for the home team announcer to view calls from his team's perspective and to analyze how it will affect them, he also has an obligation to be fair. Even if a call goes against his team, if he believes it was accurate he should say it – even if that call is accompanied by booing by the fans.

And if a call is missed – say it! I've heard Jim Jackson say, "Boy, the Flyers are fortunate – they may have gotten away with one right there." There are times when your team is hurt by a call that you're convinced is wrong and it's perfectly permissible to express your outrage.

Example:

"Boy that was a terrible call. I can't believe he's calling that! Can't he see that he was hardly touched? What an acting job!"

Show emotion – that's good as long as you're fair. Don't, however, let your criticism go overboard and never let it become personal.

Example:

"This is the worst officiating I've ever seen. Why doesn't the ref just put on a Rangers jersey?"

See what I mean? You may feel that way at the moment but try to exhibit professional restraint. In the first place it probably isn't the worst officiating you've ever seen – it just seems it in the heat of the moment. Also you never want to infer that the official is dishonest – blind maybe – but not dishonest!

INFLECTION

The tone and inflection of a broadcaster's voice convey almost as much as his words.

Jackson explains, *"If Jeff Carter's coming down with a chance to score my voice is going up – I want our audience to sense the importance of what is about to happen. Or, if a big hit takes place I want them to know just how powerful it was just by the tone of my voice. We're not the story – the game is the story, but our use of proper inflection can make the game more life-like for the listener or viewers."*

That excitement is not manufactured. All of us love our sports. We have a lot of passion. It's just a matter of allowing that passion to come out at appropriate times while keeping our descriptive techniques under control.

INSTANT REPLAY

1. Identify the players by the numbers on their sleeves.

2. Don't describe every pass in the defensive zone – use that time to update or review the scoring.

3. Never lose control even during a furious barrage of shots on goal. Clarity is a must at all times.

4. Do not berate the officials. Professional criticism of an erroneous call is fine if warranted.

OTHER SPORTS

We've covered the basics involved in broadcasting the major sports – football, baseball, basketball and ice hockey. Most of the other sports that are covered are more likely to be televised, although smaller radio stations occasionally broadcast high school soccer, wrestling, lacrosse, field hockey and even track and field competition. The determining factor for these stations is sales. If they can find a sponsor willing to pay for the coverage of a cross country meet they'll cover that also. When I was at WIP, the Philadelphia Marathon was run on the Sunday of the Eagles bye week. Naturally I found myself on the back of a flat-bed truck updating listeners on the positions of the top 15 or 20 participants. Actually I acquired related experience years earlier by doing reports for an Atlantic City, New Jersey station on the annual "Around the Island Swim". I filed those reports from a small boat that followed the swimmers.

It is impossible to become an expert on all of these sports yet it is still possible to do a good job of describing them for viewers or listeners. The key is that often repeated word again – PREPARATION.

On the network television level they have researchers who compile material to help their announcers prepare for the coverage of the Olympics with all of the different events involved. They also assign an expert color analyst who assists the lead broadcaster.

It is a mistake when covering any sport to attempt to "fake it". It just doesn't work. There's always somebody out there who will see through the bluff and when that happens you will lose your credibility even when you're covering something in which you're well versed.

It helps while growing up to play as many different sports as you can so you can at least acquire an understanding of what the athletes are trying to do. But if you have no personal experience you can still do a good job with the background study in the days ahead. Also when you work with the analyst ask any questions that you believe will give the viewer a better understanding. If you've done the basic preparation the questions will not come off as dumb or inappropriate.

Each February I enjoy watching the USA Network's coverage of the Westminster Kennel Club's Dog Show from Madison Square Garden in New York. So do millions of other viewers, based on their ratings. They devote about four hours to the coverage on both Monday and Tuesday nights. They've tried several hosts. My favorite was always former major league baseball player turned television personality Joe Garagiola. Joe was teamed with expert David Frye who has not only bred and handled show dogs but who clearly has excellent communications skills. Frye is able to speak knowledgeably about every breed and inform the viewers of what's involved in the judging process. While his words enlighten the average pet owner, they do not insult the intelligence of the dog experts. That is a rare skill. Gargiola, on the other hand, came across like the "average Joe" just having fun, and provided the perfect balance to the telecast.

There are other sports that are covered on a more regular basis by television.

All of the networks involved in golf coverage do an excellent job. This is one sport where just about everybody on the telecast is either a former player or at least a recreational player who has become very informed by a close association to the sport for many years. If this is a sport you'd love to cover you absolutely must have a golf background.

Jim Nantz, one of America's premier sportscasters and the number one man for CBS sports was actually on the golf team at the University of Houston. His college roommate was PGA tour star and former Masters Champion Fred Couples. As the anchor Nantz has been teamed with all time greats like Ken Venturi, Lanny Wadkins, and presently Nick Faldo. Nantz is an exceptional talent who also displays much warmth. Faldo, who's demeanor as a player was dead serious, now exhibits a likable, humorous, self deprecating side. Most of those covering the various holes are former tour stars. There are a few exceptions. Vern Lundquist is at the 16th hole of the Masters and he's just somebody who loves golf and plays for fun. He's also, not so incidentally, a brilliant broadcaster who has added class and professionalism to every event he's ever covered.

Dan Hicks has been anchoring NBC's golf coverage for years with hall of famer Johnny Miller. They're both silky smooth and keep the coverage flowing. They set the perfect tone and capture the significance of everything that occurs. Miller has ruffled more than a few feathers among the players for his often critical comments but he knows what he's doing and his credentials give him the license to provide these insights. Hicks is perfect in the way he sets up Miller and the teamwork between the two is something for young broadcasters to watch and admire.

ABC gave up its extensive coverage schedule but when they do carry a big tournament it's generally Mike Tirico in the anchor seat. The Syracuse University graduate is also ESPN's Monday Night Football play-by-play man, handles many basketball assignments and does a sports talk shift on ESPN's radio network. Whatever the assignment, Tirico is excellent. He, too, is a guy who enjoys playing golf and his appreciation of the sport shows.

Hard core golf fans, such as yours truly, spend hours each week watching The Golf Channel. The principle anchor for their coverage is Kelly Tilghman. She joined the Golf Channel when it began in 1995. She has also become a polished broadcaster who learned the golf side of the job first. Kelly played collegiately at Duke University before competing in Europe, Australia and Asia. She is usually teamed in the anchor booth with Faldo who moves next to Nantz when the coverage goes over to CBS on the weekends. While The Golf Channel staff includes a few broadcasters who never played the tour – all have extensive backgrounds in the sport. Rich Lerner who anchors, reports, does interviews and commentaries was a scratch golfer in his teens and a former club champion.

TENNIS

One of the real perks in this field is getting to actually experience some of your greatest sports fantasies.

As a teenager I spent many hours during the summer playing tennis. During my college years I would find summer jobs in Atlantic City that still permitted me to have time to compete in tournaments. Working as a busboy and later as a waiter at a hotel dining room was perfect. They served only breakfast and dinner. In between I either practiced or competed in local tournaments. Never did I imagine that I would one day find myself across the net from one of the sport's greatest champions – Billie Jean King. That occurred in 1974 when I became the Director of Communications for the Philadelphia Freedoms of World Team Tennis. In addition to starting the league, Billie Jean was the Freedoms' coach and number one player on a roster that consisted of three men and three women.

My job involved public relations (my journalism courses paid off) as well as traveling with the team and handling the play-by-play of their telecasts. I also hosted a pre game show with Billie Jean. Naturally I attended practices and Billie was always willing to rally with me either before or after the team began their drills. I also got to hit with Fred Stolle, an Australian who was among the top players in the world. What a thrill!

The key to handling tennis on television is knowing when not to talk. You should never speak while a point is in progress. Wait until the point is over and always give the score. It helps to be working with an expert analyst but even then the conversation should take place after points and when the players change sides of the net. Commenting on video replays is extremely important and the analyst has a great opportunity to display expertise.

In addition to baseball, basketball, football and Olympics over the years Dick Enberg has anchored coverage of Wimbledon, The U.S. Open, The French Open and The Australian Open. He conducts himself with the dignity that suits these events. His commentary is crisp, pertinent, and easily digested. He never over talks or draws attention to himself. He puts his analyst into the spotlight and, of course, keeps the focus on what is happening on the court.

Bud Collins has both anchored tennis coverage and worked as an analyst alongside of Enberg. Collins has coached the game and played at a high level but his initial recognition came from his position as a sportswriter and columnist for the Boston Globe. He began doing tennis commentary for Public Broadcasting in Boston and soon was hired by CBS. Collins developed great rapport with many of the games stars and has shared poignant human interest stories with his audience. His love for the game has always been apparent and his casual, relaxed delivery adds to the enjoyment of his audience.

Ted Robinson took the tennis anchor spot at NBC when Dick Enberg moved to CBS. Robinson is a versatile broadcaster who has both major league baseball and the Olympics in his resume. He is also the radio play-by-play voice of the San Francisco Forty Niners.

Both Enberg and Robinson have worked with John McEnroe and Mary Carillo. McEnroe is one of the greatest players in tennis history. Along with his incredible talent he was also identified with his tirades directed at chair umpires. His loud incredulous "You can't be serious!" has been replayed thousands of times and lately he has been repeating it as part of an auto rental commercial.

All of that aside, McEnroe is a superb color analyst. He says what he believes and he displays emotion. He adds an air of excitement to every telecast and is right up there with the top sports analysts in all of sports broadcasting.

Mary Carillo was actually a mixed doubles partner of McEnroe's as a teenager and like John, she displays great knowledge. She is also an accomplished broadcaster although nowhere near as emotional or flamboyant as McEnroe. She also is an excellent interviewer who uses this talent as part of the staff of HBO's "Real Sports".

I have also had the opportunity to broadcast tennis play-by-play on radio. This is something that was pioneered many years ago by England's BBC. The trick here is to follow the action from the server's vantage point. It's impossible to describe the strokes on both sides of the net.

Example:

"Roddick serves to the forehand corner – now he moves left and hits a backhand – he comes to the net – and – punches away a volley – 15 -love."

For television you merely watch the action and then add:

"Strong volley by Andy Roddick – 15-love. That was set up by the powerful serve."

When you watch the big matches on the networks, try to be aware of what the broadcasters are doing. Taking some notes and filing them away is a good idea. Don't copy their styles. Be yourself. But you can become very aware of their mechanics and the fundamentals they observe during the telecast.

SOCCER, LACROSSE, FIELD HOCKEY

Whether it's for radio or television it's important to be well versed on the names of the positions, the terminology, the rules and the dimension of the field as well as the height and width of the goals.

The basic technique in all three of these sports is the same as you use in basketball and ice hockey. You describe the passes but not every single one. Constantly update the score and the time remaining. Be clear in your descriptions.

One danger you may run into is that sometimes, especially on the high school level, there may not be much of a crowd. In the NFL that enormous roar after a big play automatically produces excitement in your voice. Conversely, if you're broadcasting a high school soccer match there could be 25 spectators scattered about. It's your job to generate some excitement – not in a phony way, but give the big plays their due. When the play goes on keep your voice interesting, upbeat and enthusiastic. You don't want a broadcast that just drones on and on or only the players' families will listen (and chances are they're at the game).

The big difference between these sports and basketball is the amount of scoring. Be prepared to add a lot of information and close up views on the players when they're deep in their own territory but as soon as they get close to their opponents goal, shift the focus back to the actual play-by-play.

Once again – it's impossible to become an expert on every sport. Don't be afraid to admit that you don't understand a ruling or that you made a mistake. Audiences will forgive you for being human but they will never let you off the hook for trying to pull the wool over their eyes.

MEN'S LACROSSE

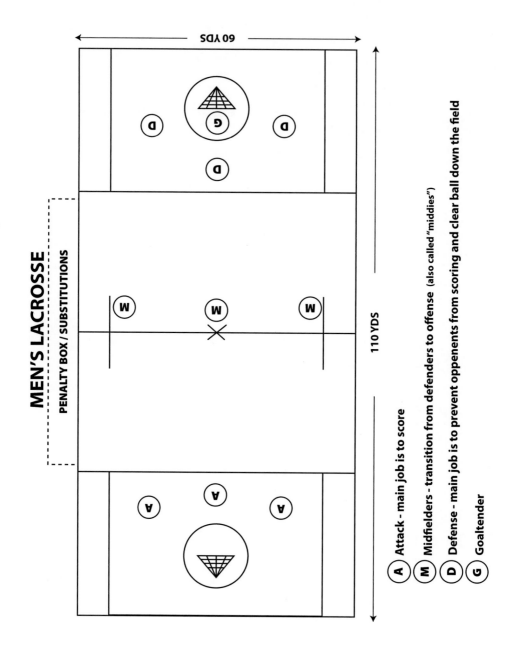

60 YDS

110 YDS

PENALTY BOX / SUBSTITUTIONS

A Attack - main job is to score

M Midfielders - transition from defenders to offense (also called "middies")

D Defense - main job is to prevent opponents from scoring and clear ball down the field

G Goaltender

94

WOMEN'S LACROSSE

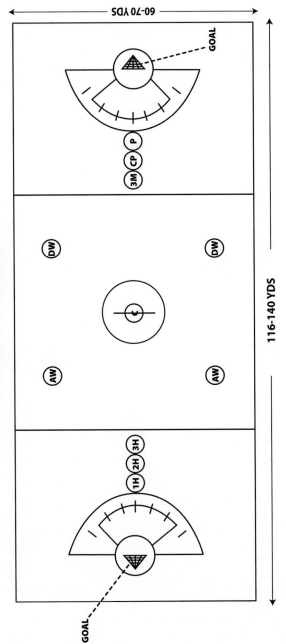

1H 2H 3H 1st home, 2nd home, 3rd home - primary shooters

AW Attack Wing - strong passers & shooters with great speed

DW Defense Wing - defenders who need to match speed of 'AW'

3M CP P 3rd Man, Cover Point, Point - Primary Defenders

G Goalkeeper

95

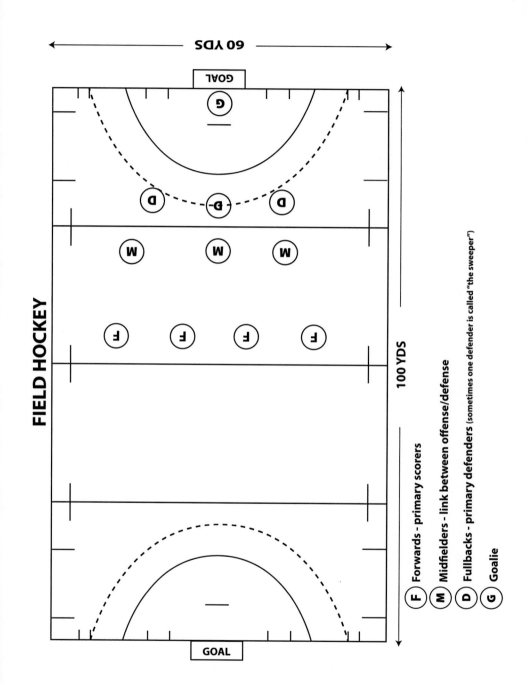

FIELD HOCKEY

60 YDS

100 YDS

GOAL

GOAL

F Forwards - primary scorers

M Midfielders - link between offense/defense

D Fullbacks - primary defenders (sometimes one defender is called "the sweeper")

G Goalie

SOCCER

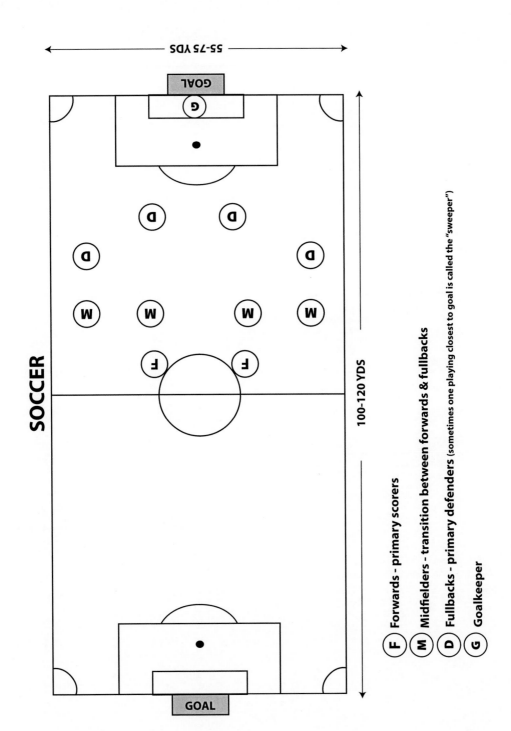

F Forwards - primary scorers

M Midfielders - transition between forwards & fullbacks

D Fullbacks - primary defenders (sometimes one playing closest to goal is called the "sweeper")

G Goalkeeper

97

INSTANT REPLAY

1. Learn everything you can about a sport before attempting to broadcast it. Get some help from players, former players, and coaches.

2. Don't try to fool your audience. You can not afford to lose your credibility.

3. Even at sparsely attended events keep your energy level high and display enthusiasm.

TELEVISION SPORTS ANCHORING

Beasley Reece

While many young people aspire to careers in broadcasting so that they can engage in play-by-play of sporting events, others aim towards sports talk radio, and still other prospective broadcasters dream of becoming television sports anchors.

They've been raised watching the anchor-people on their local stations and they've been swept away by those in front of the camera on national shows like ESPN's Sports Center.

My advice is to seek every opening regardless of which area of sports broadcasting it involves. In a field this competitive you can't afford to be specific.

While not every radio station employs sportscasters or even carries sports programming of any kind, almost every television station has at least one sports anchor. Even stations in smaller markets produce a nightly news block which almost always involves a news anchor, a sports anchor, and either a weather reporter or a meteorologist.

Many sports anchors got their initial experience on their college television stations although today many high schools provide interested students with opportunities. There are even schools that have closed circuit television with students reading bulletin board type announcements as early as 6th grade. If they continue on their path, by the time they're finished four years of college, they're very comfortable communicating and performing on camera.

Beasley Reece is the sports director and lead sports anchor for KYW-TV (CBS) in Philadelphia. He spent nine seasons playing in the National Football League where he was drafted by the Dallas Cowboys in 1976, played with the New York Giants from 1977 through 1983, and then finished his playing career with the Tampa Bay Buccaneers in 1984.

Despite the fact that Reece has the appearance, voice, poise and style of a polished professional broadcaster, many people would assume that his fascination with this field began when his days as an athlete ended and he was searching for a new career. Nothing could be further from the truth. Beasley's preparation actually began as a teenager. He remembers, "I was an Eagle Scout and one of the merit badges that I had to get along the way was in public speaking. I was in several local, state, and regional public speaking contests. That's where I started getting some positive feedback about my ability to speak to a crowd." As a junior in high school he delivered a nominating speech for a student government office. Afterwards a guidance counselor told him that he ought to consider a career in broadcasting. Beasley remembers it as "a magical moment where you have 800 students in an auditorium and I felt as if I had everybody's attention." All of that positive reinforcement raised his confidence level.

The same school counselor helped Beasley procure an internship at KWTX –Television and Radio in his home town of Waco, Texas. A legendary broadcaster in central Texas by the name of Dave South taped Beasley's voice and helped him erase the hard, southern, Texas drawl. Beasley spent hours listening and practicing and getting critiques until most of the regional characteristics in his speech had disappeared. As a senior, along with being the star athlete of La Vega High School in Waco, Beasley had two other jobs that helped shape his future. He became the editor of the La Vega "Pirates" school paper "The Jolly Roger". This helped develop his writing skills. He was also used as a student sports reporter on KWTX radio. Throughout Texas, Friday night football "rules" and the local station hired a student at each high school to phone in a live report after each game.

Beasley also happened to be his school's top player. It wasn't unusual for his report to read, "Tonight running back Beasley Reece scored three touchdowns and gained 222 yards as La Vega High School won its 4th straight game by a score of 21-7 over Moore High School. Reece opened the scoring with a 95 yard kick off return. Reporting from Downingtown Stadium in Waco, Texas – this is Beasley Reece." Because of his dual role Beasley became a real favorite. He then starred in football at North Texas State where he majored in journalism.

Naturally that perfect background came into play when he took advantage of television opportunities both as a Giant and as a Buccaneer. In Tampa he let everybody know that he was pursuing a television career. When an opening occurred he was ready.

WHAT IT TAKES

Believe it or not, every television performer isn't a natural extrovert. Off the air some people actually possess a more reserved nature. But if this is your goal, you do have to enjoy performing and have a talent for story telling. Nobody looks into a television camera and immediately feels at ease. Beasley Reece says, "It takes a long time to become comfortable – really comfortable. You have to be so comfortable and confident on the air that what comes through to viewers is a person they feel completely at ease with welcoming into their homes." The lens and microphone only magnify any feelings of insecurity. That's why it helps every broadcaster to get as much experience as possible in a small market. Beasley points out, "The first five years I was nervous to point where I would keep a little towel within reach just in case my brow became wet with perspiration while I was on. When I was off camera for a moment I would dry my forehead. I had to work my way through it. The way I survived was by repetitive work. It took me five years of doing this night after night until I reached a real comfort level. It sure doesn't happen over night regardless of your background." Technical problems can trigger some real panic for the inexperienced broadcaster, "You worry about how you'll react if the video you've just introduced doesn't appear. The first few times it happened I didn't handle it well. Nobody does. But along the way you learn to get through that and you simply smile, shrug your shoulders, and say 'Sorry, we don't have that right now, but we'll cue that up just as soon as we can.' You go through that a few dozen times and it becomes no big deal. But in the beginning, in the early days as a television anchor, it's almost an initiation that we all endure."

EYE CONTACT

Just as eye contact is a key for a successful public speaker, it's a must for a television performer.

Beasley Reece points out, "I learned eye contact by staring into the lens and having very little movement. Every movement is magnified on the television screen. Gradually I increased my movement slightly. My goal was for every movement to appear natural. If I moved my head I wanted it to be the kind of movement that I would make if I were sitting across from somebody having a conversation."

Another way of learning eye contact is by observing television anchors who appeal to you. Don't copy their style but learn from their fundamentals. Watch the natural, smooth way they move from one camera to the other, and the way they nod to emphasize a point. This is something that can be learned with practice and can actually be improved upon by looking into a mirror. Today there are so many experienced anchors to learn from with all of the national sports programming available. If you want to be an athlete you watch those who are the best in the world and try to emulate the aspects of their games that you are capable of incorporating into your game. It's unlikely that you can duplicate Tiger Woods' club head speed but you can watch how he lines up a putt and see if it works for you. It's the same with a television anchor you respect. Check out his or her posture, eye contact, movement and see if it will improve something in your overall presentation.

With athletes there are certain truths that I've learned over the years. No coach, no matter how knowledgeable, can teach somebody to run fast. He can help his athletes get the most out of their ability – make a fast runner a bit faster - but somebody with average speed will never become fast. It's the same with a quarterback or pitcher as far as arm strength. The quarterbacks with the rifle arms and the pitchers who throw blazing fast balls were born with that talent. You can improve accuracy and work on mechanics.

It's the same with a person's voice. You can teach articulation; you can explain how the voice should come from the diaphragm – not the throat or nasal cavities. You can polish and improve but basically a voice is a voice. The great John Facenda who generations of football fans heard narrating dramatic features for NFL Films had that incredible resonance that could make you feel "the frozen tundra in Green Bay". That was John Facenda's voice – and not a result of anything he was taught.

On the other hand a smooth, professional delivery can be learned and developed with hard work. Beasley Reece refers to reading a teleprompter as an art. Originally he worked with a script with large type that was actually scrolled just beneath the camera lens. He had a pedal that he pressed to control the speed. Now the teleprompter is computerized but there is still a technician operating a toggle switch which determines the pace. There's teamwork involved. The two people work closely together and the technician has to develop a feel for the announcer's tempo.

The technique employed to sound natural while reading a teleprompter is the same as what you use while reading any script – read ahead. The seasoned professional will actually have his eyes a couple of sentences ahead of what is coming out of his mouth. If you focus on each word as you are saying it, your presentation will be very choppy and unnatural. Beasley suggests, "This sounds very complicated but it's not. You can practice this by taking any book or printed article. As you read try to focus on one or two words ahead of what you're saying. As you become more and more comfortable increase your word span. Eventually you'll actually get to the point where you can be a sentence or two ahead with no problem."

This works, believe me. That's how you can read without stumbling. Your delivery will develop a real flow and it will sound totally natural. This will also enable you to provide the right emphasis on words and the proper inflection.

They're all tied together. There are times when you may pause to set up a big point. Your pitch and volume should be varied – the same way they are when you're engaged in a conversation with a friend. It all starts, however, when you develop the technique of reading ahead.

WRITING & PREPARATION

Television sportscasters are generally responsible for writing their own scripts. Actually in the entry level jobs in small markets they pretty much have to be a jack of all trades. They shoot their own videos and then come back and do their own editing. At the larger stations this is done for them but they still have to script their sportscasts. That's where any journalism or creative writing courses in college come into play. There are certain basics, certain fundamentals that should be observed. Remember, however, that you are writing for the ear not for the eye. That's why the text in this book may seem a lot less formal than what you're accustomed to reading. I've been writing for my own broadcasts and telecasts for so long that it's natural for me to be less formal. That's why I use so many contractions. In an article someone might write, "You are going to see a great game." On the air you'd say, "You're going to see a great game." Write the way you speak. Your script should always be an extension of your personality.

Unless Beasley Reece is out covering a late breaking story he arrives at the studio for the Channel Three 4pm newscast at about 3pm.

Most of that sports segment is assembled by a group of 7 or 8 producers. Beasley does prepare his own script through a computer program called INEWS. He enters it directly and it is instantly ready for the teleprompter when he delivers his sports segments.

Early in the day Beasley carefully scans the sports sections of every area newspaper. He also has several favorite sports web sites that he examines. His producers do the same and rarely is there a story that warrants coverage that slips through the cracks. Occasionally Beasley will become aware of a local story in his area and he'll text message a producer requesting that they send a video crew to an event. This could involve a high school team about to break a state record or a local athlete achieving something extraordinary.

   After the first sportscast Beasley meets with the producers and they decide the order and emphasis for the 5 o'clock, 6 o'clock and 11 o'clock shows. After he gets off the air he returns to his desk, checks the next day's schedule of events and as the clock strikes 12 heads home for a good night's sleep.

LIVE REPORTS

Today almost every television sports anchor is called upon to do what is commonly referred to as a 'live shot'. This is a report that is done from a remote location where an event is either being held or was held or will be held. This gives the viewer the impression that the sportscaster has the latest information. It works really well when you can actually see players warming up in the background. For an inexperienced broadcaster this can be a very unnerving experience. Beasley Reece remembers his early days of dealing with live shots, "You tend to want to memorize what you're going to say so you write down every word of your report. You become a slave to that script." Beasley then progressed to writing down a key word or a key phrase that sparked a memory. There's nothing wrong with the reporter looking down at his or her notes from time to time. Actually there's nothing wrong with looking down and reading from time to time. This gives the viewer the impression that you're simply trying to be factual. Now Beasley Reece and most of the top experienced sportscasters simply look into the camera and tell a story. They have enough confidence in their knowledge of the subject to simply ad lib. Still, they think through and carefully plot their report before the red light goes on. The last thing you want to do is wander and beat around the bush. The report should be just as factual – just as comprehensive regardless of whether it's scripted or not. If the director tells you that he has a sound byte, make certain that you're clear and authoritative when you lead into it.

When doing a live shot you really have to concentrate. You never know when a player with a sense of humor will come over and try to distract you or attempt to make you laugh. If the team has just won a title, be prepared to get something poured over your head. It happens all the time so just relax and enjoy the celebration. In fact, Beasley says, "You pray for things like that because it makes the viewers at home feel that I have a good relationship with these guys!"

You do worry about getting too close to the crowd at an event because you never know how certain fans are going to react. The FCC is very strict about airing obscenities and you do not want your station to incur a fine. Beasley has actually turned to nearby fans prior to a live shot and told them to call their families so that they can see them on camera. You remind them that this is family TV and they should have a good time. The experienced reporter will actually warm up that crowd and turn what could be an embarrassing situation into a positive. He suggests, "You shake a lot of hands, you pump a lot of fists – you make friends with them so they don't ruin your shot. They have a good time because they're on television. Crowd management is huge!"

TEAM WORK

The television sports anchor is part of a team with both the other air talent and the technical crew. That includes the person controlling the teleprompter. In the large stations the producer selects the video highlights and tells the anchor which ones to script. Of course if the anchor and producer work together they can share likes and dislikes and get on the same page with their preferences.

There's also the teamwork involved with the newscaster and the meteorologist and others who may be part of the telecast. It's important to develop at least a cordial off the air relationship with these people. Any tension between performers has a way of coming through. That's the last thing you want. The objective is for the viewers to feel relaxed and comfortable and to develop a sense of loyalty to your news – sports team. Regardless of which network they're watching prior to your show – when it's time for the news you want them switching to your channel. That will only happen if they practically consider you part of their family.

The one thing that can lead to tension more than anything else is the air time allotted for each segment of the news show. It's natural for everyone to feel as if they warrant more air time. Truthfully, you can't control that. Only the producer or the news director can. You can make a case from time to time if you believe that you have a really important story (a major trade involving a local team, a championship game, an unanticipated firing of a head coach) but once the decision is made – live with it. That's the mark of a true professional. Nobody agrees with every decision that's made but in the long run the person who can handle these things in stride, who can view them as philosophical differences, or business decisions – not as personal attacks will be a lot happier and ultimately more successful.

Instant Replay

1. It takes a great deal of experience to feel truly comfortable in front of a T.V. camera.

2. Work on eye contact by keeping as still as possible while looking into the lens.

3. Reading a teleprompter smoothly involves focusing your eyes ahead of the words coming out of your mouth.

4. Write a script with an informal style. The words should sound as if you're having a conversation.

5. On a "live shot" look into the camera and tell a story. It is permissible to look at notes and read when necessary.

SPORTS TALK RADIO

Al Morganti

Angelo Cataldi

Rhea Hughes

*Philadelphia's
Sports Talk Radio 610/WIP*_____

Life was less complicated for great athletes in earlier times. Even those who became household names like Babe Ruth, Red Grange and Jack Dempsey could find some privacy when they needed it. They were larger than life figures but were still judged mainly by what they did on the diamond, field, or in the ring.

Throughout the years that privacy became a little harder to find, especially with the advent and growth of television. Players became involved in the advertising industry and became recognizable from their identification with certain products. Joe DiMaggio, the legendary "Yankee Clipper" became instantly identifiable to a whole generation who never saw him swing at a pitch because he came into homes every day as the spokesperson for "Mr. Coffee", an electric coffee maker.

When I first started broadcasting Eagles games in the late 1970's there was no denying the popularity of the NFL. Commissioner Pete Rozelle led the league throughout a period of skyrocketing success.

While fans began to fill stadiums and both radio and television ratings soared there was nowhere near the all consuming focus on our heroes that is so prevalent today. The reason, in my opinion, can be traced to something that hit America on July 1, 1987 - SPORTS TALK RADIO. It started on WFAN in New York and has been going strong ever since in every city.

The idea of a radio show on which a host discusses various sports topics with listeners was nothing new. That, and issue oriented news talk shows had been going on for years. But, the idea that a station could go 24 hours a day, seven days a week focusing only on the world of fun and games seemed improbable.

Prior to all-sports stations, fans would still debate the strengths or weaknesses of the home team's quarterback or whether the manager of their baseball team had any chance of leading that team to a World Series. But now this conversation lasted all day, every day! Fans became so focused on these issues that they became actual factors in a player's state of mind.

I can remember the 1999 NFL Draft – the first for Eagles Coach Andy Reid. While Reid believed that the team had to use its number two overall pick in the first round on a franchise quarterback, the fans of Philadelphia felt differently. By and large they wanted University of Texas running back Ricky Williams. Philadelphia's Sports Talk Radio 610/WIP spent hour after hour airing opinions and analysis. Their morning host, Angelo Cataldi, is a former Eagles beat reporter for the Philadelphia Inquirer.

Angelo led the Ricky Williams bandwagon and often aired live conversations with then Mayor Edward G. Rendell (now Governor of Pennsylvania). Rendell went so far as to urge fans to bombard the Eagles switchboards with telephone calls demanding that the team draft Ricky Williams. Cataldi went one step further. He organized a group of fans, deemed them "The Dirty 30", and led them to the actual spectators gallery at the NFL draft headquarters in New York. When NFL Commissioner Paul Tagliabue announced, "With the second selection in the draft the Philadelphia Eagles select quarterback Donovan McNabb of Syracuse University." "The Dirty 30" let loose with loud raucous booing.

In truth, they were not booing Donovan McNabb. They were booing the decision by Andy Reid and Eagles management to draft anyone but Williams – the guy they were convinced would single handedly lift this franchise to the Super Bowl title they long coveted.

This is something Donovan McNabb has never forgotten. From his vantage point it's understandable. Here's a talented young athlete who dreams about the day he gets drafted into the NFL. When the moment finally occurs, when that dream reaches fruition what does he hear? Booing! I can understand exactly how he felt. On the other hand sports talk hosts don't become successful by being perfectly reasonable, mild mannered, non inflammatory gentlemen. They are molders of public opinion – they beat the drums and stir the pots.

Almost every coach and every athlete will tell you that they don't read newspaper sports pages nor listen to radio sports talk shows. But, somehow, some way they seem acutely aware of everything that's written or said.

Sports talk hosts come in all shapes and all sizes. They also come from a wide range of backgrounds. There are those who have traditional broadcast backgrounds. They majored in communications and received their first experience on a college radio station. Next they beat the bushes until they found a small commercial station willing to give them an opportunity. Chances are that they did everything – disc jockey shows, newscasts, talk shows, engineering and very possibly sales. Finally, when their skills were polished and their confidence had been bolstered they applied to a larger station, went through an audition process and were given that "opportunity of a lifetime."

Many of today's top talk show hosts have journalism backgrounds. They achieved notoriety either as beat reporters or columnists for newspapers. They knew their subject matter and they were comfortable interviewing sports figures. Most sports-writers are also used to being interviewed by broadcasters on halftime shows or serving as panelists on various pre and post game shows. Those who display a spark, a charismatic personality, or exhibit a great sense of authority are often offered opportunities to try their hand at broadcasting. Many of the best have been lured away from their newspaper jobs. Some have managed to balance both careers.

The quickest way to broadcast stardom is to achieve fame and fortune as an athlete. Broadcast outlets are always interested in somebody who will bring instant credibility and increased advertising to their various shows. The list is long of former professional athletes who finished their playing careers and moved directly into the booth or the studio. Unfortunately, the list is also long of those who didn't last once their fame as athletes faded. But those who had natural communications ability and worked hard to develop those talents endured. Some even achieved greater success off the field than on it. Hard work pays off regardless of which route you take.

In the sports talk radio field there are some unusual stories. New York's WFAN's midday host Joe Benigno started out as a passionate sports fan who loved to call the station and converse on the air with the hosts. He worked in food sales but his all consuming interest was sports. In 1994 WFAN held a fan appreciation day and several fans were invited to go on the air. From that, Joe was given a one hour live audition and came through with flying colors. Next came part time work as a fill in host. Finally, he got his biggest break when he was given a full time shift. New Yorkers know that he's one of them – that he lives and dies with their teams and they feel as if they're spending time with a friend. The Joe Benigno story is certainly unusual but it can happen. One other thing – when Joe first started getting some opportunities he enrolled in a broadcasting school. He wasn't content to just let nature take its course. He worked for everything he achieved.

Marc Rayfield is the Senior Vice President and Philadelphia Market Manager for CBS Radio. You will never meet a more passionate sports fan. While this passion didn't lead him to a career in front of a microphone it is evident in the way that he leads WIP – one of the nation's most successful sports talk stations. Marc climbed the broadcast ladder through the sales side of the business but he admits that his love for sports is something he leans on to get through the tough days that all high level executives endure in intensely competitive, pressure packed industries. "Early on," Rayfield relates, "I drew some criticism for not dividing my passionate fan side from the business side you most adhere to."   Marc's first love has always been baseball but until the Phillies moved to their new park and their subsequent on-the-field success, Eagles football dominated sports talk in Philadelphia 12 months a year. While Marc, the baseball fan, would have enjoyed more balance between the two sports he understood that allowing a radio station to reflect your personal tastes is a recipe for disaster. He also could not let himself become emotionally involved in the opinions of his on-the-air hosts. His job was to head a highly rated, successful radio station not provide an outlet for Marc Rayfield sports fan!

Andy Bloom is the Operations Manager of three major CBS owned Philadelphia radio stations including Sports Radio 610/WIP. His background includes many of the top stations in America. Bloom knows that a life long love of sports is the first thing any sports talk host needs. Several of his top hosts have newspaper backgrounds, "Journalism classes provide an excellent background. Being a good journalist makes you a better broadcaster. It teaches you to speak in crisp sentences, use better grammar. If you write well, you learn to speak well." For a while there was a trend of hiring writers for sports talk but that has leveled off. That's one source but now there's more variety. Most sports talk hosts are either home grown or have lived in the area in which they broadcast for a long time. Says Bloom, "They really have to have a passion for the teams in their city. They have to care deeply about whether they win or lose and about the future of those franchises."

Bloom adds that even those who were hired with strictly print media backgrounds had to develop broadcast skills along the way. I always believed that one of the key ingredients that a successful sports talk host needed was an argumentative nature. Bloom disagrees, "I don't think that all of our successful hosts are argumentative. Some are, and it works well, but others are more likely to let somebody state their opinion, point out that they're entitled to that opinion, state that they disagree and then punch the button and move on to the next caller. Occasionally, they'll get a caller who is so off the wall that the host can't help blowing up and displaying some real emotion." Still there are hosts who have built careers by using a short fuse to create excitement but Bloom sees that changing, "It's all cyclical. We live in a difficult time in America and in the world. People do not want to listen to some-body scream at them. I think that they would much rather have an entertaining, interesting dialogue and not have the heated debate. We're in the part of the pendulum swing where it's a little less desirable right now to have a full fledged argument on the air. People are more receptive to listening to an entertaining debate rather than one that transmits bad feelings on both sides. This is a trend that broadcast ratings reflect nationwide."

Sports talk hosts must have highly developed senses of humor. They must have the ability to laugh at themselves. Many great hosts will be absolutely convinced that their opinion is correct but in the sports world there are many surprises. The team that was picked to lose by three touchdowns can pull off an upset and the baseball manager who was thought to be a bumbling idiot can take his team to a championship. The best broadcaster won't try to justify why he delivered the wrong opinions. They laugh at themselves. They admit that they were way off base – that they were wrong. They show their human side and when they do, they become so much more likeable and listenable.

PREPARATION

Like every other form of broadcasting meticulous preparation is a must. The host should be totally informed as to what is going on locally and nationally in the sports world. In this day and age it's easy to zero in on what's being written and said across the country. The top sports publications should all be thoroughly scanned. There is no excuse for being blindsided by something written in a local paper that you didn't see. You do not read that paper while you're on the air. It's fine to reference it if you want to be certain that you have the right quote but showing up without having digested all of the important stories is unacceptable. In this field, "The dog ate my homework" simply doesn't cut it!

Every sports talk host should also have access to any statistical or background information that might be needed. Laptop computers make this easy. There's no longer a need to carry 48 media guides and record books into the studio for every show.

The host also has to have a pretty good idea as to where that day's show is headed. You can not depend on callers to make or break a show. Bloom points out, "Sports shows are reflections of the hosts. They reflect their personality, their demeanor, their passions. They can't fake it. If they don't really care about a certain sport the listeners will know. As Rush Limbaugh says, the purpose of the caller is to make the host look good. The caller sets up the host so the host can display knowledge and insight. That's what the calls are for. The calls move the host through the show."

There's no doubt that sports talk radio shows provide a real service for the sports public especially after an excruciating loss.

It allows them to get off steam and to commiserate with other fans who have suffered the 'slings and arrows' connected with the 'agony of defeat'!"

Still, the shows revolve around the hosts. The truly skilled broadcasters could arrive at the studio, learn from the engineer that the phones aren't working and that all they'll have in the studio is a microphone, and still go on. They would merely shrug their shoulders and then proceed to inform and entertain for the next four hours. That's what being an exceptional talk radio host is all about. The hosts who depend on callers to keep their shows entertaining are soon looking for other lines of work. Remember, the host conducts the callers, sets the tone, controls the tempo and uses the callers to enhance what he's trying to accomplish.

SINCERITY

A sports talk host should be sincere when he voices opinions. Andy Bloom says, "I think you can tell when somebody is trying to do something on the air for affect. Sometimes they're really driving a point home, and they're going over the edge and they're really pushing it but if it is not at their core belief, if they're insincere, if they don't truly believe what they're saying I don't think they can be successful. Now they may exaggerate the point, they may become cartoonish for entertainment value, and to create an effect, but that's fine. That's 'theater of the mind' great radio, but I do believe they remain true to their core values."

Often sports talk hosts are paired for two person shows. They seem to disagree on many issues which makes for more interesting radio. That happens basically because most program directors attempt to pair people who are total opposites. You don't need hosts to second each other's motions or support each others' line of thinking. It's fine if they agree from time to time but if they're almost always on the same page, the combination clearly isn't working.

TEAM AND PLAYER RELATIONS

There's a fine line when establishing rapport with owners, general managers, coaches and players. It is the job of sports talk hosts to critique what they see at games. There are some hosts who choose to stay far away from the locker room scene. They may inadvertently get to know a player or two because of the nature of their business but they never want to become friends with anyone connected with the team. They're afraid it could impair their ability to view things impartially, with an air of detachment. If the host is a highly opinionated, somewhat controversial figure in that city because of his "no holds barred" style, life could be very uncomfortable if he chooses to become a locker room regular. It's the same with becoming very close to managers or coaches of a team. Certainly there are benefits. You will receive privileged information. There are stories you are fed that nobody else has. Every reporter and every broadcaster loves to break exclusives. But with that relationship comes certain responsibilities. You are expected to be less harsh with your criticism and always give those connected with the team the benefit of the doubt.

Andy Bloom addresses this issue: *"I've worked with hosts who are on very opposite extremes. This is a very, very difficult issue. I believe there is a happy medium between never attending a practice and being so familiar with the people involved that you are treated as part of the family.. I think it's important to have some insight that goes beyond what you see from the press box or on television. That insight comes from professional relationships. On the other hand, I'm fairly certain that your opinion and judgment can get clouded if you become too tight with an organization. I think having the ability to obtain information by asking a question on an 'off the record 'basis is good but I think there's a line that should be respected. Every broadcaster, every journalist has to be able to look in the mirror and ask, 'Have I been objective? Have I been able to criticize players and management with whom I have a relationship. Have I been able to evaluate them both positively and negatively without allowing my personal feelings to get in the way?'"*

This is something that every broadcaster or journalist has to decide for him or herself. How close is too close? Are you standing too far from the arena to the point where your vantage point is no greater than the fans? The fact that you have a microphone and a position in the public eye gives you a responsibility to obtain and divulge some firsthand information.

If your criticism is honest, if it's justified, if it's sincere then in your position you can't worry about the team's reaction. If you violate confidences that's another story. If you've been given confidential information with the understanding that it is not to be made public, respect that. Use it to enhance your understanding and add to the insight that you provide to your audience.

PUSHING THE RIGHT BUTTONS

It is the aim of the successful sports talk host to stir the passions of the audience. You must know what their biggest concerns are and you must be able to keep their fire burning.

When a team makes an unpopular move sports talk radio stations get a boost in their ratings. On February 28, 2009 Philadelphia Eagles safety Brian Dawkins signed a lucrative contract with the Denver Broncos, ending his 13 years with the Eagles. Dawkins was the longest tenured athlete in Philadelphia and one of the most beloved sports figures in the city's history. He was much more than just an outstanding football player. He was the guy reporters went to for comments involving any significant occurrence affecting this team. His words were always uplifting, his attitude always positive, his tone inspirational.

The moment it became known that Dawkins was even visiting the Broncos, Eagles fans went wild. This is when sports talk hosts rode the wave and kept those phone lights blinking for days on this subject alone. Some quickly jumped on the organization accusing the front office of everything from being cheap to showing no regard for their loyal fans. Others defended the move and said that it was a tough football decision but never-the-less time for them to bolster their defense with a younger, faster, player.

Regardless of the stance that a host takes it should be full of sound reasoning and delivered with a large heaping of emotion.

The sports talk host is not a college professor conducting a semester. He's part reporter, part commentator and at all times an entertainer.

Up Close and Personal

There are sports talk hosts who allow listeners into their personal lives. They talk about their families, their health, their favorite foods, their vacations – about many aspects of their off-the-air goings on. I have even heard broadcasters in the course of a sports talk show share the pain of an impending divorce with their audience. The audience really gets to know this person and develops a very personal attachment.

There are other hosts who keep things very business-like. They reveal next to nothing about their personal lives. At the same time their show is upbeat and entertaining and eagerly anticipated each day by a large audience.

Then of course there are those who fall in between. They may mention their spouse's name from time to time when it pertains to the subject matter at hand and they may refer to a non sports related experience but that's as far as they go.

There is no right or wrong in this area. There are hosts who have been very successful with any of these approaches. The one thing I will stress is that when that microphone is on you must always be professional. The quality of your show should not be affected by how you feel either physically or emotionally. For the three or four hours that you're on the air you're a performer. Like the great athlete, you must be able to shut your personal problems out of your mind and focus solely on doing the best show possible. Consistency is a key to success in anything. You should strive to make each show riveting – a good show three out of five days is not enough. Obviously some days are better than others for a variety of reasons but there is no excuse for a dull, preoccupied performance.

Cow Catchers

It is the goal of every sports talk host to hold on to the audience as long as possible. One of the ways to accomplish this is to keep promoting an upcoming story or guest. You can even be somewhat vague about when that guest will appear.

Example:

"Matt Ryan will join us sometime in the next hour to tell us what his first year in the NFL was like. You won't want to miss that later this morning."

Going into a commercial break you should always make certain that your audience has their appetites wet.

Example:

"We're headed into a break right now but after we return you're going to find what's going on in Dallas that could backfire in the Cowboys' faces."

When you're back on the air or you can mention that story again and still get to it a little later or you may choose to deal with it right after the break. Remember the longer you can extend the listeners the higher your ratings are going to be, however, don't let the listeners hang too long or they could get frustrated and tune away. Experience will help you develop a sense of timing.

PROMOTIONS

Rarely can a sports talk host sit down and come up with an exciting original promotional idea. It is generally something that arrives on the spur of the moment.

Andy Bloom tells us, "Most great promotions grow organically. They start out as something small pick up steam and explode! Ideas pop up when you least expect them."

One of the most successful promotions in sports talk history is WIP's "Wing Bowl". It began in January of 1992 after the Eagles had been unceremoniously knocked out of the playoffs by the Dallas Cowboys. Morning show producer Joe Weachter remembers the show's host Angelo Cataldi and cast members Al Morganti and Tony Bruno sitting around after the show bemoaning the fact that once again there would be no Super Bowl appearance for the Eagles. The two week wait for the game between Dallas and Buffalo seemed interminable. They were thinking about some kind of a contest involving listeners. Morganti mentioned that with the Bills being in the big game maybe they could do something with Buffalo Chicken Wings. Weachter always had a knack for coming up with catchy names for promotions and offered "Wing Bowl" as the perfect event for the Friday before Super Bowl Sunday.

Weachter remembers, "We only had two weeks and we made up the rules as we went along." Two listeners volunteered to take part in this eating contest to be held in the lobby of a center city hotel where the morning show took place every Friday. The day arrived and Cataldi, who is a charismatic entertainer, built the proceedings to a fever pitch. Morganti's glib, sarcastic sense of humor provided the perfect balance and Bruno was ideal for slipping into the role of the play-by-play announcer to capture every bite. The station program director was skeptical of this creating any real interest. The only prize he could come up with was a Budweiser Party Kit that included a hibachi barbecue grill, an apron and a hammock.

The winner of this two man battle was Carmine Cordero Jr. He devoured 50 wings in the first six minutes of the half hour event and coasted the rest of the way. Right after the Super Bowl there's a quickly produced commercial in which the game's most valuable player is asked, "Where do you go from here?" The answer is always, "To Disney World!" Bruno posed the same question to Carmine Jr. only to be told, "I'm going to Wing Bowl Two." Wing Bowl II? This was only intended to be a one time event. Unexpectedly it got such tremendous audience reaction that it's been going strong ever since and its growth has been remarkable.

Wing Bowl is now held at The Wachovia Center – the home of the 76ers and Flyers and each year over 18,000 fans pack the building to view the event. The number of contestants has grown from two to anywhere from 25-30.

The station begins promoting the event on the Monday after Thanksgiving. They hold on-the-air eating stunts to select contestants and they also have "wingettes" – cheerleaders to inspire the eaters and certainly entertain the crowd. The winner now receives prizes that include an automobile (a far cry from a party kit) and the radio station sponsorship sales exceed a million dollars.

Wing Bowl may not be a true sporting event but the business of sports talk radio in most cases now involves a lot more than just sports. WIP's leader Marc Rayfield points out that the event has achieved national notoriety – even among people who have no knowledge of his station.

The Wing Bowl

INSTANT REPLAY

1. Sports talk hosts must have a feeling for and knowledge of the local teams.

2. Displaying passion and emotion from time to time evokes response from your audience.

3. Having rapport with athletes, coaches, and team executives helps you acquire inside information but don't get so close that it compromises your objectivity.

4. Sustain interest in your show by leading into commercial breaks by promoting upcoming topics and guests.

5. The best promotional events begin as spur of the moment ideas.

THE ART OF INTERVIEWING

Almost every on-the-air job in broadcasting involves at least some interviewing. For those involved in sports broadcasting it is a very, very important skill to acquire.

While most areas of broadcasting have improved over the years, I actually believe interviewing techniques have regressed. Interviewing for radio and television at its best is simply a revealing conversation. The listener or viewer actually has the feeling of eavesdropping and acquiring very interesting information. The skilled interviewer acts as an emissary for those in the audience. The questions posed are the ones that those in the audience would ask if they were able to speak with that subject.

Throughout the history of radio and television there have been some remarkable interviewers. There are many great ones that you can learn from that you see quite often. Their style may be different from what you would feel comfortable with because we all have different personalities which come out in an interview. Watch somebody like Mike Wallace who can be very aggressive and at times exhibits almost a court room manner. Barbara Walters, on the other hand, is disarmingly friendly and has been able to extract very personal information from world leaders to Hollywood stars. Larry King made the transition to television from radio without batting an eyelash and his line of questioning is always so natural. ABC's Diane Sawyer is upbeat, self assured, and conveys the perfect tone to any interview. One of my favorites of all time was the late Johnny Carson of "Tonight Show" fame. He knew how much involvement he needed. If he had an entertaining guest he might just add a word like "really?" here and there but if the guest was a real dud he would pick things up and provide the spark and get more involved in the discussion. Jon Stewart of "The Daily Show" exhibits many of these same outstanding qualities.

In recent years more and more print journalists have made the transition to the electronic media. Many of them have become excellent broadcasters. They've used the expertise gained by covering something closely and have honed their oral communications skills. There is, however, one remnant from their days with the written press that I believe is a negative. As sports-writers they had firm deadlines. They're used to bursting into a post game locker room, filling their notebooks or recorders with quotes and heading back to the press room to compose their stories. They have little time for idle conversation. It's not unusual to hear them ask the player who drove in the winning run, "talk about the 3-2 pitch that you lined to left field", or ask the manager to "comment on Moyer's performance." They need quick snippets of information and they need it fast. That's rarely a requirement in radio or television and yet time and time again I'm aghast as I hear broadcasters (many without newspaper backgrounds) say to a guest, "Talk about your goals for this season", or "Comment on what you thought was the turning point of the game". The second I hear that, I realize that I am not listening to a good interviewer. Instead of the former writers learning from broadcasters, too many broadcasters have unwittingly fallen into the writer's mode.

A broadcast interview, a good one, is supposed to be a conversation between two friends or at least two acquaintances. When is the last time you turned to a friend and said, "talk about what you ordered for lunch", or "Comment on your plans for tonight". It just doesn't happen, and it shouldn't on the air either. Listen to any of the outstanding interviewers that I mentioned – listen to somebody like Bob Costas or NBC's Jimmy Roberts and you'll never hear that. Instead you'll hear a warm, informational conversation.

One of the most successful broadcasters I've ever met is somebody I grew up listening to and watching in the Philadelphia area. With the exception of Flyers hockey, Bill Campbell has broadcast just about everything. Eagles football, Phillies baseball, Warriors and then 76ers basketball are all in his background along with college football and basketball, the Penn Relays and almost everything else you can think of. Bill and I have become close friends and when I've been fortunate enough to sit down and discuss broadcasting with him I feel as if I'm attending this profession's version of a "master class". Bill Campbell interviews over the years have been almost magical. They seem absolutely effortless. At no time do you ever have a question you wish had been asked. He's been doing this since 1940 and yet he's as fresh and enthusiastic and at the top of his game as ever.

Connie Mack and Bill Campbell

As a 23 year old reporter Bill was at Shibe Park to report on a Philadelphia A's American League baseball game. The A's legendary owner – manager Connie Mack called him over and asked if he could handle the public address announcements since the regular P.A. announcer was ill. In those days all the P.A. guy did was announce the starting lineups and pinch hitters or pitching changes. Bill finally summoned up the courage to ask Connie Mack for an interview (which was broadcast live) and a recording of it remains in the baseball archives. To this day Bill refers to the baseball pioneer as "Mr. Mack" and he remembers Mack calling him "Mr. Campbell". As a matter of fact, he even addressed his players as "Mr. Joost", etc.

Things today may be a lot more casual but the fundamentals of effective interviewing haven't changed. Bill says, "The guy who coined the expression 'Brevity is the soul of wit' really should be canonized. All good interviews, the ones that you remember contain short, uncomplicated questions. You make the guest feel comfortable. The listener never wants to hear your opinion when you're asking a question. Unfortunately there are so many interviewers so intent on displaying their knowledge of a subject that the questions are long, winding and confusing. By the time the interviewer turns to his guest he has trouble figuring out what the question is. People see us and hear us a lot. They want to hear what the guest has to say."

That's great advice. The preparation I've emphasized in every area of broadcasting is once again a key. If you're well prepared there's no need to show off your knowledge. It'll come through in your line of questioning. I must admit that interviewing is something that did not come naturally to me. When I first started I used to fear that I would ask a question, receive an answer and draw a blank. To eliminate that possibility I actually scripted my interviews. I wrote out each question and made certain that I had enough to fill whatever time frame I was allotted. If that's what it takes to make you comfortable initially do it. The interviews may sound a bit stiff but it's a lot better than stumbling around figuring out what to ask next. After awhile my confidence grew. I took the next step and began putting a brief outline on a three by five card. This acted as a guide and kept me on course. Gradually I found myself departing from these notes and asking questions that came to me in the course of the interview.

This led me to the final step. I now go into an interview prepared and with a well thought out plan of what I'd like the interview to accomplish. All great interviewers have one thing in common – they're great listeners. They learn to formulate their questions from their guests' responses. Like any other skill – this takes time to develop. Don't rush it. It will come. Don't be afraid to use the script or note cards until you feel totally confident. A lot also has to do with your guest. If that person is somebody with whom you're friendly it's a lot easier.

There's nothing more frustrating than tuning in to a radio interview that is already underway and not knowing who the guest is. In television that problem doesn't exist because you can see the guest and also because graphics are usually used to identify the people on the screen.

To avoid this problem on radio it is important for the interviewer to re-identify the guest every few minutes. He can simply insert the line, "I'm speaking with Baltimore Ravens coach John Harbaugh" or simply lead into a question by saying, "John Harbaugh, next week when your team meets the Colts..."

This will keep your listeners from getting frustrated and tuning out.

PRE GAME SHOWS

Before I became the Eagles play-by-play man I handled the pre and post game shows for five years. Each day during the season I would spend time in the team's locker-room after practice chatting informally with different players. Only after I developed a rapport with a player would I ask him to appear as a guest on the pre game show. In the off-the-air conversations I would learn things that sparked really interesting responses when we eventually did go on the air. Also I got a real feel for which players would make the most entertaining and informative guests. That comfort level that you need for an exceptional interview can't be over emphasized. I learned that early when I decided to interview a rookie receiver who had been making some impressive catches at training camp. I really didn't know him well but I knew the fans would want to hear from him. I asked him a well thought out question to begin our ten minute segment. His answer was simply, "Yes." When he answered my second question with, "No." I knew I was in trouble. Believe it or not he actually answered one question with a shrug of his shoulders which doesn't make much of an impression on radio. Somehow, someway I managed to live through that experience. That player, Harold Carmichael went on to become one of the greatest wide receivers who ever played. By the end of his career he had become a relaxed and eloquent speaker and is now in charge of player programs for the Eagles in which he councils young players on their off the field activities. He's also a close friend with whom I could probably sit down, turn on a recorder, and fill an hour's programming with no trouble whatsoever.

POST GAME SHOWS

Post game shows are different. Here you rarely have very much time to prepare because they're right after the game and the guest is often a player who had a significant role in the games' outcome without any regard to that player's verbal ability. Still if you're a good listener you might just strike gold. Bill Campbell remembers such an occasion after the Braves had defeated the Phillies in Atlanta. "My guest was Braves' third baseman (and now prominent manager) Joe Torre. Torre had hit two home runs in that game. During a commercial break Joe actually suggested that I should ask him about the curve ball he jumped on for that second home run. I took his advice and then just listened as he told how he actually saw the bat make contact with the ball on that hit. Imagine he hit a curve ball that was thrown at about 80 miles an hour and he actually saw the ball hit the bat. Torre pointed out that the great Ted Williams sees that happen three or four times a month and that he's only seen it happen twice in his career. It was absolutely fascinating stuff for baseball fans and I will never forget it."

On a post game show you have to understand that the athlete, no matter how cooperative, wants to get back to the locker-room where the rest of the press corps is waiting, grab a shower or get treatment and then leave the stadium or arena. Generally on the post game show your questions should be related to what just occurred or what is ahead in the immediate future.

Bill Campbell recalls a post game interview with Hall of Fame pitcher Sandy Koufax after he threw a no hitter against the Phillies at Connie Mack Stadium. "I tried to make it as quick as I could out of respect for all of the other reporters who were waiting for Sandy. He gave me a remarkable interview that went on for seven or eight minutes. While we were doing it, Chris Short who had been the Phillies pitcher that night walked past us in the dugout to get to the locker-room. Koufax nodded towards Short and said, 'If I had that guy's arm they might never hit me.' Sandy, despite his dazzling talent, was suffering with arthritis in his left arm. Short smiled. A few seconds later a batboy appeared with a cold beer for Sandy and said 'This is from Chris.' It was a priceless moment."

One of the common problems you might have to face on post game interviews is player availability. It is not unusual for a TV crew to charge onto the field and grab the player for whom you're waiting. Some coaches insist that the players assemble for a quick post game meeting before they're available to the media. In this case you must be prepared to fill with pertinent statistics about the game or scores from around the league – anything until the player arrives. Do anything you can in this case to avoid going back to the station for a commercial or updates because invariably once you take that break the player will suddenly appear. The last thing you need is an impatient player standing around for three or four minutes until you can reacquire a live microphone. If it does happen simply apologize, engage the player in conversation and hope that he understands your situation.

LOSING LOCKER ROOMS

Doing post game interviews after a win is easy. Spirits are high and most athletes enjoy talking about their triumphs. Unfortunately there's also the other side.

On the Eagles post game show we interview Eagles after wins, losses, and in the case of what occurred in Cincinnati on November 16th, 2008 a tie. I have a system for selecting guests. After a win you have a lot of options. There are a bunch of players who enjoy going on the air and receiving kudos for what just happened. There are losses and there are losses – they're not all the same. There are times when a team plays well and simply is outmanned against a stronger team. There are other times that a team plays poorly and loses to an opponent they should beat 9 out of 10 times. There are other losses that come at critical times in the season or in playoffs and championship games. These are the toughest for everyone to endure and obviously getting players to go on the air and discuss it is very tough. That's when I call on friends. While I try to establish rapport and have at least a casual relationship with every player on the roster there are always 4 or 5 with whom I actually have developed a friendship. These are usually veteran players who I've known since their rookie seasons. Many I've had the opportunity to golf with in the off season and I've also worked with them at various charity functions. I will rarely go to one of these players after a win. I save them for the most difficult circumstances. You never want to wear out your welcome – to go to any player too often. I know that if I'm really in a difficult spot there are several friends who will rescue our post game show.

Even with these players respect their situation. Never put them in a position where they're forced to comment about the performance of a teammate or a controversial decision of a coach. There's enough to focus on if you stick with discussing the turning points in the game, their analysis of what their opponents were doing and what the team needs to do to bounce back. I'm not implying that a post game interview after a loss has to be trite and predictable. You can still extract some real substance from the interview without making the guest uncomfortable in a very difficult situation.

COACHES SHOWS

Hosting a coaches show can be fun. It can also give you an opportunity to foster your relationship with the coach. It all depends on the coach. Some love to do these shows. Others would rather walk across a bed of nails. Some coaches enjoy taking live phone calls from fans. Others wouldn't dream of subjecting themselves to what could turn out to be second guessing and abuse. There are some coaches who participate in these shows for one reason – they're obligated through their contract with the team.

It doesn't matter. If you show the coach respect and earn his trust you can turn this into a very informative and listenable show. You can't do this if you have an adversarial relationship with the coach. That doesn't mean that you have to avoid tough questions or areas that could be sensitive. I try to have at least a few minutes of off the air conversation with the coach before the show actually begins. I might prepare him for what's ahead. There's nothing wrong with saying, "Coach, I've got to ask you about your decision to punt in the 4th quarter." When you ask it on the air don't beat around the bush and don't precede it with your opinion. Once he answers it don't challenge him on his response. This is not the job of the host on the coaches show. Leave that up to the sports talk hosts. They'll have a field day putting each key moment, every significant coaching move under an intense spotlight. That's their job. It's not yours. But, if you're honest, straight forward and respectful you can handle the most difficult shows while maintaining your rapport with the coach and your popularity with the fans.

Over the years I've had some difficult situations to handle but none that compared with what occurred near the end of the 1998 NFL season. The Eagles were in the throes of a terrible season. Head Coach Ray Rhodes was in the fourth year of a five year contract but the handwriting was on the wall. After losing their first five games it was obvious that unless this team suddenly came to life Ray Rhodes was finished. I could see the strain in his eyes each Monday night as we met at a steak house for his live one hour show. Things continued to go wrong – injuries – fumbles – penalties – all the things that come along with losing. Rumors were rampant. Actually they were more than rumors that the Eagles were shopping for a new head coach. As they approached their final game with their record at 3-12, newspapers were already speculating as to who the next Eagles coach would be. Ray's fate was sealed. Never have I covered or worked with a finer gentleman than Ray Rhodes. Even after the most bitter defeats he never took out his frustration on those around him. He actually asked our producer to allow the most critical calls to get through. He enjoyed going back and forth with Eagles fans and more often than not by the time the conversation was over they had become Ray Rhodes fans.

The last game of that season was at home against the New York Giants. It occurred to me that we also had one final coaches show – the Monday night after that game. It was also clear that by show time he would be the former head coach of the Eagles. On Thursday, December 24th, Christmas Eve day, my knees wobbled as I knocked on the door of his office in the bowels of cold, grey Veterans Stadium. Ray invited me in and he could immediately tell that I was troubled. I asked him what he was going to do about that final show. "We'll do it, or course," he said. Then he paused, looked up and said, ""Oh, I see what you mean – I'll be fired by then." I suggested that rather than put himself through that we could tape the show right now and act as if it were Monday night and the parting of ways had already occurred. He jumped at the opportunity. I pushed the record button and began, "Ray, today you learned that you will not be back as the Eagles coach" and on we went from there. He couldn't have been more professional as he thanked the Eagles ownership for the opportunity, he thanked the fans for their loyalty, and he reminisced about the highs and lows of the past four years.   As we ended the show tears began to run down his cheeks. He gave me a big bear hug. As I left the office I became very emotional and I realized once again that I had just been in the presence of a very special person. The rapport, the friendship that had grown over the past four years was the key to making what could have been an impossible situation workable.   In fact, it was an experience I will never forget.

COVERING A BEAT

Sal Paolantonio has been covering the NFL for ESPN since 1995. He actually was a highly acclaimed political reporter for the Philadelphia Inquirer from 1985 through 1993 and authored a best selling book about legendary police commissioner turned mayor Frank Rizzo. In 1994 he welcomed the opportunity to cover the Philadelphia Eagles as a beat reporter and to take a role on a nightly Inquirer television show. The assistant sports editor at the time, Jim Cohen moved to ESPN in Bristol, Connecticut as a coordinating producer and the following year he convinced Sal to join their staff.

Sal Paolantonio

Sal says covering a political campaign and covering an NFL team can be very similar and both can be uncomfortable at times. He points out, "It's like knocking on your neighbor's door, sitting down and having coffee with them, asking them to divulge their family secrets, turning around and broadcasting it to the world and then going back the next day and expecting the same kind of hospitality." Covering politics proved to be an excellent background for covering sports. It taught Sal how to generate and cultivate sources and divulge information so that readers would know what is going on. At the same time it is necessary to refrain from violating the privacy of the individuals involved. He realized that information received confidentially was not for public consumption but it could be extremely useful in enhancing his understanding of a situation. It paid off in future reports. The biggest difference, according to Sal, is that politicians want to talk to you while coaches don't. Politicians often use the media to gain publicity and to get a message across. Coaches are much more guarded with the behind the scenes happenings of their teams.

Sal's job in going from city to city covering 32 teams is a lot different than that of the reporter who covers one team and becomes a familiar face in the locker room. Sal is conscientious about expressing gratitude to everyone he interviews. He sends out hand written thank you notes. Sal recalls, "I was recently asked by Jets linebacker, Bart Scott, why I did that. I explained that I'm going into your workplace and you're giving me your time and I want to convey my appreciation." Scott said he had never received a note like that from any other reporter.

Sal always asks players first if they would mind answering a few questions for Sportscenter. He never just walks over with a camera crew, extends a microphone and begins firing questions. But once the interview begins and the player or coach is aware of what the interview is for, it is not the reporter's job to save somebody from a controversial response. Players today go through media training and are advised by team public relations professionals on what areas to avoid. Once your interview begins they're on their own. During the 2009 season, Sal spotted Eagles wide receiver DeSean Jackson in his car in Moorestown, New Jersey. He remembers, "He was in front of the post office. This was right after the game in which he suffered an injury against the Washington Redskins. He honked and we rolled down our windows. I asked him if he was going to play in the next game. He said that he wasn't. He said that he had blacked out. That was the first time he had detailed his injury. I asked if I could quote him saying that he had blacked out and he said that was not a problem. I actually went back to him before releasing my report just to make certain that since he had suffered concussion symptoms he was aware of the information he had given me. Showing that extra concern further fosters a solid relationship for the future."

Sal teaches a sports journalism course at St. Joseph's University in Philadelphia. He offers this advice to his students, "Ask open, neutral, lean questions. An open question begins with WHAT, HOW or WHO for the purpose of eliciting information. A lean question is succinct. Don't go on and on. A neutral question avoids trigger words or sarcasm. By doing this you will avoid one or two word responses.

It's very important to look for the change in the status quo. How did what transpired change the game, the season, or your career? That response will make news and become memorable by its significance."

Sal also preaches what he refers to as his "Three P's" – PREPARE – PROFESSIONAL – PERFORM. "There is no substitute for thorough, meticulous preparation. This will greatly aid in your confidence which will be instantly conveyed to the person you are interviewing.

Act professional which also means dress professionally and treat people in a professional way.

The performance Sal stresses is also enormously important. You can have a good story filled with information but if you can't communicate in a manner that captures your audience it will not make an impact. In the interview the tone with which you pose the questions is as important as the responses. The interviewer must exhibit an air of confidence. He can not come off timidly. The broadcast journalist must be capable of informing his audience in an entertaining, captivating manner.

INSTANT REPLAY

1. Keep questions brief.

2. Be conversational. Never, never, never tell a guest to "talk about" something.

3. Establish a rapport with guests if possible. Save best guests for more difficult situations.

4. On coaches shows – treat the coach with respect. Prepare him for what's coming and never challenge his responses.

5. When covering a beat, establish mutual trust with the people on whom you report.

PUBLIC ADDRESS ANNOUNCING

"Gola goal!" "Dipper dunk!" "Two for Shue!" "And now from the University of Massachusetts – Julius Errrrrrrving!" Those were just some of the trade mark blasts that rumbled out of the mouth of the late Dave Zinkoff. "The Zink" as he was affectionately known by generations of Philadelphians was the man you heard when you visited old Convention Hall or the Spectrum. He was as famous as any of the Warriors or 76ers. Zinkoff also did public address for the Phillies early in his career and he was the traveling secretary and voice of the Harlem Globetrotters. The road leading in to the South Philadelphia sports complex bears the sign Zinkoff Boulevard.

The public address announcer is not a broadcaster in the true sense of the word. Other than in the background he is not heard over the air. But for those who attend sporting events he is basically the master of ceremonies. While the best broadcasters are electronic journalists, many of the top public address announcers are entertainers.

Their styles vary greatly from the often hilarious Zinkoff to the extremely dignified Bob Sheppard who welcomed fans coming to see the New York Yankees and the New York Football Giants. During a time out in a basketball game Zinkoff was not above making a prank announcement – "Will the owner of a green Buick with the license plate 646CL please report to the parking lot. Your lights are on – the doors are locked – and the motor is runnnnning." And of course the crowd roared. Public address announcers become icons in a city. John Condon was the voice of basketball at Madison Square Garden in New York. John Ramsey was the stadium voice for both the Los Angeles Dodgers and the football Rams when they resided in Los Angeles. Nobody was more of a fixture at a stadium than the late Pat Piper who started at Wrigley Field in Chicago in 1917 and worked the Cubs games for almost 60 years. When Piper began there were no booming sound systems. The announcer merely turned towards the crowd and spoke loudly through a megaphone. Sherm Feller was as much a part of Fenway Park as "The Green Monster".

Dan Baker

Unlike play-by-play broadcasters, many P.A. announcers do this work in conjunction with other jobs. Obviously, they do only a team's home games and they are generally paid by the game. Still, Dan Baker, the stadium voice for both the Phillies and the Eagles says there's nothing in the world he would rather do. Along the way he taught school, served as the executive secretary of Philadelphia's "Big 5" college basketball and is presently the Coordinator of Broadcast Relations at Drexel University. Dan remembers playing sports as a youngster and after scoring he always mimicked Dave Zinkoff. During his college years Dan got a job in the mailroom of a local television station. While there he met Buddy Wagner who ran an auto daredevil show. He hired Dan and for three summers he toured as the voice of the show which played at one county fair after the other. Dan also got hired to do statistics for many visiting sportscasters when they came to Philadelphia.. While at the stadium Dan met Pat Cassidy who was the director of operations for the Phillies. Prior to the 1972 season Cassidy alerted Dan to the possibility that the team could be looking for a new public address announcer. Dan remembers, "One of the jobs of the P.A. announcer at Veteran's Stadium was to operate the game in progress board. (balls, strikes, outs, runs, hits, errors). You don't have to be a rocket scientist to do it but you do have to pay very close attention. It's easy to be distracted because you're working with a lot of people. You can't lose your focus for a second." Dan's interview for the job was with Phillies vice president Bill Giles. Dan promised Giles that if he got the job he would be the quickest and most accurate scoreboard operator in baseball. Dan believes to this day that was a major factor in getting him the job. For the thirty two years that Dan worked at Veterans Stadium nobody in baseball was quicker or more accurate. Of course, Dan Baker is also an exceptional P.A. announcer with a much admired distinctive style. Once the Phillies moved to their gleaming new stadium, Citizens Bank Park, the scoreboard operation was computerized and it is no longer the responsibility of the public address announcer.

Bill Giles was also a showman who was looking for someone with a real flair and Dan's background with the auto daredevil shows was also viewed as a positive.

Dan wouldn't trade his job for that of a play-by-play broadcaster. "I love the connection with the live audience. I can see that audience and immediately experience their reaction." While there is an aspect to performing involved Dan advises aspiring P.A. announcers, "You are not the show. You are here to provide a service. You're an aid to these fans. Be concise, and be accurate. While there are times when you can add life to an event and accent a memorable performance, be direct. Get in and get out. Don't stay on the microphone for too long."

Dan displays a great deal of versatility. He often descends to field level where he addresses the crowds as a pre game host. Earlier I mentioned that years ago the P.A. person rarely mentioned more than the absolute basics. That role has certainly grown. There are often pre game events and promotions taking place. Dan simply remains on the field and delivers the starting lineups from there. One day the Phillies held a birthday party for the Philly Phanatic, their widely recognized mascot. Dan was asked to wear a costume as he emceed the festivities. Other nights there are presentations to be made from the field. Three games into the 2009 season Dan presided over the elaborate ceremony in which the Phillies received their World Series rings. His dramatic delivery greatly enhanced the festivities.

While I have rarely done any public address work there have been several occasions when I've had to rush down to the field at halftime to make a presentation to a former Eagle being inducted into the team's honor role. It can be very confusing speaking into the public address microphone and hearing the echo of your voice booming back at you. Dan Baker says, "The trick is simply to ignore it. Just speak as you would under normal circumstances – at the same pace. If you listen you'll only become confused. This is something that national anthem singers go through all the time. That's why hours before the fans enter the stadium they have the singer rehearse with the sound system turned up to the game time level. It's something you will get used to. But it is something that requires practice and experience.

PREPARATION

The preparation that is necessary for success in any aspect of broadcasting is just as important in public address work. First and foremost is knowing the correct pronunciation of every possible name that you may announce. Most team media guides and many team game day releases contain a pronunciation guide with the name spelled phonetically. There's only one problem. Few people who write these are actually schooled in phonetics and therefore the way they attempt to sound the name out in print may be incorrect. The best way to get the pronunciation right is to stop by the broadcast booth and see the visiting play-by-play man long before he goes on the air. He is an authority on the team he covers. In New York, Bob Sheppard would always stop by and ask for my assistance and I was always happy to provide it. Everyone respects a person who is meticulous in his preparation and conscientious about every aspect of his job. The ultimate authority for how a name is pronounced, of course, is that person himself. Early in Dick Vermeil's tenure with the Eagles he signed his former Rose Bowl quarterback from UCLA, John Sciarra. With the Eagles John was primarily a punt returner and a safety. Dick pronounced his last name Shy ra. I checked with John and he told me it was actually pronounced Shar ra with the emphasis on Shar. Sometimes players actually change the pronunciation of their names after they get into the league. When running back Tony Dorsett entered the NFL after a great career at the University of Pittsburgh his last name was pronounced DOR sett with the emphasis on the first syllable. He later requested that the emphasis be placed on the second syllable and he became known as Tony Dor SETT. There was even a former New England Patriot whose name was Mike Taliaferro. He pronounced his last name Tolliver. Actually former Redskins' quarterback Joe Theismann pronounced his last name Theesman all through high school. While at Notre Dame the director of sports information Roger

Valdiserri asked him to change the pronunciation so that his last name would rhyme with Heisman and influence the vote for college football's most prestigious award. Joe never won the Heisman. Instead it went to Stanford quarterback Jim Plunkett.

ADDING TO A POSITIVE ATMOSPHERE

Sporting events can become very emotional. Crowd control can become a major problem. There have been riots and near riots all over the world that began at what was supposed to be competition between two teams. No doubt you've read about some frightening scenes at soccer games in Europe. But much closer to home we're all aware of fights which occurred in the stands during baseball and football games or of spectators throwing bottles and debris onto the field.

The public address announcer has the responsibility to keep the tone of the event as positive as possible. He will naturally be more dramatic and exuberant when introducing the home team or when identifying a member of the home team who scored the touchdown or basket or goal. That's fine, but he should never do anything to embarrass an opponent player.

In the NBA there's often a show business atmosphere. At 76ers games spectacular dunks are often accompanied by the sound of glass being shattered with the voice of public address announcer Matt Cord rising to the occasion. When an opponent scores Matt deliberately low keys it. He doesn't make fun of the player, but the casual identification is just part of the show.

Dan Baker had a difficult situation the first time J.D. Drew came to town as a member of the St. Louis Cardinals. Drew was the Phillies top draft choice the previous year. The Phillies were unable to sign him and there were a lot of bad feelings on both sides. In his first appearance in the on deck circle there was a real uproar from the Phillies fans. When he came up to bat, Dan Baker announced Drew's name. Baker was criticized by ESPN announcers and some other reporters for stirring up the crowd. Baker disagrees, "The crowd was already in a negative uproar.

I did say his name louder than I said the others. I did it because the crowd was already booing J.D. Drew and I had to raise my volume in order to be heard over the crowd – not to provoke a negative response. The crowd's behavior was frightening. There were even some batteries thrown on to the field." At that time Baker's role took on added importance. He remembers, "At that point home plate umpire Ed Montague called me and told me to get on the P.A. mike and warn the crowd that if anything else is thrown the Phillies will forfeit the game. I was worried that if I made too strong an announcement it would only provoke the crowd into worse behavior. The first thing I did was call Philllies president David Montgomery. Dave gave me his clearance. I then got on the mike and made the announcement as diplomatically as possible. I focused more on potential injuries. Chastising the crowd would have been a major mistake. I said that we didn't want any players injured. I never used J.D. Drew's name because that would have only thrown more kerosene on the fire. I mentioned the possible forfeit and then things began to quiet down. My tone was very low key, very matter of fact – it had to be or we could have had a real disaster."

Dan Baker finds football more difficult from a public address standpoint. At the Eagles' Lincoln Financial Field he works with his son Darren who serves as a spotter. That's similar to the process that the play-by-play broadcaster employs. On the other hand he must avoid actually lapsing into play-by-play. He provides only the essentials.

For example:

"Kolb's pass – complete to Jackson – a gain of 15 yards – tackle on the play – DeAngelo Hall. First down!"

That's it – rarely a full sentence – just a caption to what the fans watched with the identification of those involved. There are no adjectives. An experienced P.A. announcer will display a flare but he will not become the show.

The public address announcer is also apprised by the team public relations department before the game of any records which the team or a player may be approaching so that he will be prepared to recognize them if they occur. He must wait for official word from the team before announcing the records to the crowd. The statistics that he keeps are not official. His announcements of records are also coordinated with those running the stadium video screens so that the announcement coincides with what is seen.

Today many NFL teams employ multiple public address announcers. While Dan Baker handles the in game football information and some other messages, a separate announcer is on hand to provide a theatrical presentation of the starting lineups. Players no longer trot out of the locker room tunnel. Today they emerge through huge inflatable helmets or clouds of smoke and many have their own dance or signature way of coming on to the field. This is an age of entertainment and while the athleticism displayed is greater than ever so is the show business element. There's even a third announcer, usually a local disc jockey wearing a team jersey down on the field to handle various promotions.

The public address announcer in hockey also has an exceptionally demanding job. The Philadelphia Flyers announcer, Lou Nolan, has held that position for over 30 years. He works closely with the officials and the official scorer. Because of the speed of the sport he must wait to receive word of the goal scorer and also the player credited with the assist. He also confers with the officials before announcing the penalties after they are enforced.

Oops

Any person who has performed in athletics or on the air or in front of a crowd has experienced moments he'd like to forget. The public address announcer rarely has as many embarrassing moments as the play-by-play person because he says a lot less. He speaks in short spurts. Still – things can happen. Years ago Dan Baker was introducing Phillies outfielder Willie Montanez to the crowd at Veterans Stadium. For some unknown reason Dan announced "Now batting for the Phillies – Number 27 – Willie McCovey" (McCovey played for the Giants.) He couldn't believe that came out of his mouth but those things happen. Not often. But they do occur when you least expect them. The second he said it Montanez stepped out of the batters box and looked up at Dan. The next day Dan saw Montanez before the game and the two men had a good laugh but at the time it occurred, Dan wanted to crawl under the desk in his booth.

A baseball P.A. announcer must be very careful late in the game when multiple lineup changes are made both in the batting order and on the field. The last thing you want to do is confuse those at the stadium.

The key to a smooth performance is concentration. Never allow your mind to go on "automatic pilot". Even if a game is one sided and has long ago lost its competitive drama it is your job to stay on top of everything that is happening and present the same up beat, professional delivery to the crowd.

INSTANT REPLAY

1. The public address announcer is the stadium or arena master of ceremonies.

2. Announcements must come in short spurts.

3. Ignore the echo which comes back in delay from stadium speakers.

4. Make certain that all names are properly pronounced.

5. It is part of your duty to aid in keeping the crowd from becoming unruly.

OVERTIME

I've thoroughly enjoyed writing this book. It gave me an opportunity to sit down and speak with a lot of top professionals who I truly respect. There are so many things that you do in the execution of your job that become automatic over the years. It's good to actually pull things apart and evaluate all of the ingredients that comprise a successful career.

Regardless of which aspect of this field I was examining there were many common threads. The first word out of everyone's mouth was the same – preparation. Nobody gets anywhere worthwhile in this business by faking it. In sports I have seen some incredibly talented athletes squander what should have been hall of fame careers. Buddy Ryan used to tell me, "I don't want players who just want to win. Everyone wants to win. I want players who are prepared to pay the price that it takes to win." This is not just one of those corny old adages that is part of what is commonly known as "coach speak". There's so much truth to that. Just as I've seen athletes fall far short of their potential, I've seen broadcasters do the same. They're more intent on having a great social life and turning every day into a party than they are in focusing on their career. There's nothing wrong with having some balance in your life. There's a time to relax and enjoy some diversions. But this profession is tough. A very small percentage of those who target sports broadcasting as a profession actually hit the bull's-eye. Those who do connect have varying degrees of natural ability but they have one thing in common – the drive. Not a day goes by when they don't try something in an attempt to get ahead. This is their number one priority. It has to be. They also can't expect to make a decent living early in their career. If you make enough to eat and pay the rent you're ahead of the game. The financial rewards are certainly there but they come much later. Don't worry about how many hours a week you work, how much vacation time you get, or what the retirement benefits are. Just get that first job and make the most of it. Regardless of what you're assigned, go the extra mile. When I was doing news early in my career I wasn't content to just slap together a newscast and read it on the air. I was always searching for somebody to call – to get as many sound bytes as possible in order to make that newscast come alive. I put endless hours of preparation into a high school sporting event. I never took the attitude that since this was just a stepping stone job I'd get by with the minimum of preparation. The top professionals pushed themselves to be the best at the beginning of their careers and they maintain that attitude throughout their lives. Dick Vermeil once told me that in football, players either get better or they get worse. They don't stay the same. It's the same in broadcasting. After 33 seasons of broadcasting Eagles games I still strive to improve. Every summer prior to the start of the pre-season schedule I have the station send me CDs of 6 games. I listen to them from beginning to end and really dissect them. I look for phrases that I repeat too often. I search for ways to describe certain formations with greater clarity. I sit there with a pad and jot down note after note. I don't beat myself up and hang my head but neither do I puff out my chest and feel satisfied. Complacency is the enemy of any professional, in any walk of life. Don't ever let it stymie your development.

LOOK THE PART

   While more emphasis is given to the physical appearance of a television performer than to a radio broadcaster that doesn't mean that the voice that isn't seen can be oblivious to grooming and attire. Every broadcast organization wants people who represent their station well. Never show up to broadcast a game in an old tee shirt and a pair of ripped jeans. I realize this sounds old fashioned and my son and daughter would probably give me a tough time. But truthfully – if you want to be a professional, dress and act like one. That doesn't mean that you have to show up for a high school basketball game looking as if you just stepped out of G.Q. But, you also shouldn't look like a member of the student body. I realize that things are a lot more casual today than they were in years past. Still – check out the way the sports broadcasters and anchors are dressed on television. Whether you like it or not there are certain industry standards. If you aspire to reach those heights you must subscribe to them.

RELIABILITY

In broadcasting you can not be late for your job. There are no excuses. None. Absolutely none! A broadcast goes on the air at a scheduled time. This is not a job where you can arrive a half hour late and then just stay an extra half hour to make up for it. You shouldn't even play it close. The few broadcasters that I've known who have taken chances and come in at the last minute eventually slipped up and missed the start of a show or a game. When that happened they generally lost their jobs.

I leave the house for a one o'clock Eagles game at 8:30 a.m. I want to know that if I get four flat tires on the way to the stadium that I can still figure out a way to get there in plenty of time. I know that sounds extreme but nobody who rushes in at the last second and jumps behind the mike is ever going to be prepared. In my football chapter I told you how I prepare once I get to the stadium. The other broadcasters do the same – Harry Kalas watched batting practice, Marc Zumoff is at the shoot around, Jim Jackson doesn't blink during the pre-game skate. Dan Baker carefully goes over each pronunciation. Bill Campbell took time to develop rapport with the players before they went on the field. The top talk show hosts are at their desks checking the important stories of the day or reviewing video of a game they intend to discuss. The only time Beasley Reece races into the TV studio is when he's just coming back from covering an event. Of course, rather than do that he'll do a "live shot" from the event if it's possible.

There are also few excuses for missing an air assignment. Illness is one thing over which we have no control but weather is never a legitimate excuse. Like the proverbial mailman – neither rain, snow or sleet should ever keep you from getting to the studio or to an assignment. In my days at small stations if the forecast was ominous I would drive to the station the night before and sleep on a sofa rather than risk being snowed in at home. The day be-fore the Eagles met Atlanta in the 2004 NFC Championship game the snow started falling. Before the ground was covered I drove to a hotel near the stadium. The last thing I needed was to spend the night worrying about a possibly harrowing drive to the stadium the day of the game. Any responsible broadcaster would have done the same thing.   This is a business where "the show must go on" – it's that simple.   If you're worried about how many sick days you get and whether or not you have to work on holidays you're choosing the wrong profession. There isn't one of us who hasn't worked on every possible holiday. It's part of being a professional broadcaster.

THE MICROPHONE IS ALWAYS LOADED

More broadcasters have lost their jobs by uttering profanities on the air than you can imagine. In most cases this occurred when they thought their microphone was off and that they were not on the air. As I'm sure you've heard on blooper tapes, there were moments of great excitement when in the heat of the moment the announcer utters something he never realized he said. The Federal Communications Commission does not take kindly to obscene language whether it is uttered intentionally or not. The station over which it is aired is subject to a large fine.

I have a rule for those involved in our Eagles broadcast. Once you enter the booth, even if it's hours before air time any questionable language ceases. That prevents any inadvertent problems. Remember even hours before a broadcast the engineers may be engaging the microphones for test purposes. All it takes is for somebody back in the station control room to have a switch in the "on air" mode and anything said is broadcast. It's no big deal if an occasional "testing one, two, three" goes out but if the wrong words are picked up, everyone involved is in big trouble.

As far as the heat of the moment stuff – I've heard broadcasters whose off the air vocabulary is rather salty. I'm not about to make a moral judgment but the fact is that if certain words are part of your everyday speech pattern you run the risk of an inadvertent faux pas on the air. While most broadcasts are in a protective 7 second delay, it is hardly unusual for a studio engineer to miss pushing the delete button.

Again, I would not tell anyone how to speak in their private lives but I choose to use the same language off the air as I do when I'm behind the mike. That doesn't mean I won't utter an unmentionable when I miss a two foot putt but my normal vocabulary is acceptable in a family setting.

THE CARE AND FEEDING OF YOUR VOICE

The most important tool you have is your voice. On radio, of course, the voice is the sole means of communication. On television play-by-play most of the time you're off camera and it's your voice over the video. While the TV sports anchor can also communicate with facial expressions, a clear authoritative delivery is extremely important. The voices of sports talk hosts come in all pitches with various regionalisms. Some have used a thick accent to their advantage. Christopher Russo and Mike Francessa who for years teamed on WFAN in New York sound like New Yorkers through and through. Russo is now with Sirius Satellite Radio where he signed a lucrative contract.

Whether your voice is rich, resonant and mellow or distinctively quirky it still has to be at its best for your broadcast assignments. Take care of it. I have a few rules that I follow the day before an Eagles game.

1. **Stay out of noisy environments.** On the road it's not unusual after dinner on a Saturday night to gather in the hotel lounge to relax and chat about the upcoming game. If it's quiet, that's fine. But if there's a band or loud music I stay away. There's a natural tendency to talk over the noise and that puts tremendous strain on your voice. You need it for at least three full hours the next day – you can't afford to wake up Sunday morning with a sore throat or with hoarseness.

Even at home on a Saturday night if my wife, Cindy, and I are going out for dinner during football season we'll choose a restaurant which we're sure is quiet.

2. **<u>Stay off the phone.</u>**   This is not something I made up. I actually read it years ago in a book by the legendary hall of fame broadcaster Red Barber.

I know it's not possible to avoid all phone calls but the night before the game I keep any phone conversations very brief. There's a tendency to project differently on the phone. Lengthy phone conversations can tax your vocal cords.

3. **<u>Get a good nights sleep</u>.**   I'm not a great sleeper. Normally during the week, six hours is plenty. It's not unusual for me to stay up late watching a game on television and end up with considerably less. But not the night before an Eagles game - I try to get a solid seven hours. Actually, if the Eagles are playing a night game I try to nap for an hour or two in the afternoon. It really refreshes me and adds greatly to my vocal stamina.

4. **<u>Do not eat or drink dairy products right before the game.</u>** Stay away from milk or ice cream right before the game. Dairy products tend to produce mucus. It will cause you to constantly clear your throat. I keep cold water or soda next to me in the booth. It helps to constantly lubricate my voice. One warning – don't use too much ice. This can freeze your tongue and contribute to sloppy speech.

5. **<u>Don't yell!</u>** The day before the game is not the time to turn into a fan. Even if your child is playing in the game, resist the temptation to cheer too loudly or to shout instructions across the field. Trust me – if you become too vocally exuberant you'll pay for it the next day.

While broadcasting - try not to show your excitement by raising your volume. Even during exciting moments experienced broadcasters will transmit that excitement with changes in pitch and inflection – not volume. Our engineer will tell you that the VU meter on his consol remains pretty constant for the entire broadcast.

PERSONAL APPEARANCES

Young broadcasters should look for every opportunity to make personal appearances. It's nice if you can find some that reward you financially but that shouldn't stop you from doing some without compensation.   I probably make five charity appearances for every one that involves an honorarium or talent fee.

It's interesting how a broadcaster who is heard by thousands of listeners every time he opens his mike can have trepidations each time he thinks about addressing a luncheon or dinner meeting. That's natural. It's something almost all of us went through. After years of doing this and appearing at hundreds of events I still get what I refer to as pre game jitters. The more public speaking appearances you make – the more comfortable you'll feel. It also helps you connect with your listeners and it helps you enlarge your audience. Don't get consumed by the nervousness. It simply means that something is very important to you. If I didn't get butterflies before an Eagles broadcast I'd think something was very wrong. As our producer gives us the "30 seconds countdown" I can feel that bass drum beating in my chest but the second he cues me it all goes away and I feel as if I'm floating in a zone for the next three hours. It's a great feeling. Whether it's a speech or a broadcast those jitters contribute to a real sense of energy.

One warning. When appearing at a live gathering follow the same rules that you subscribe to during a broadcast. If you have inside information or if you're protecting a source don't feel as if you can open up just because you're not on the air. Believe me – even if there are only 30 people at a luncheon it will still get out once you say it publicly. I found out the hard way years ago when some candid comments that I made at a small business breakfast appeared in the organization's newsletter the next month.

SALES VS. PROGRAMMING

   As strange as this may sound there are sometimes strained feelings between the sales and programming departments of both radio and television stations. The sales people are out to make as much revenue as they possibly can. The program people, including the talent, are out to produce the best broadcast possible. While they understand the necessity of commercial intrusions, they generally feel that sales goes overboard with their demands. I can understand both sides.

   When I first started broadcasting Eagles games over 30 years ago there were no live commercial reads in the broadcast. All spots were recorded and were played only during an official time out on the field. There were no commercial promotions like "the drive of the game" (brought to you by a car dealer), or "the catch of the game" (sponsored by a seafood restaurant). There was no "bone jarring hit of the game" (sponsored, of course, by a medical center). If the people in sales can dream up a commercial tie-in with some facet of the game, rest assured they'll sell it.

   There was also a very small rights fee that the station paid the team to become its flagship radio station. Players salaries have greatly escalated and one of the team's most important sources of revenue is the broadcasting and television rights. With the increased cost of carrying the games it is necessary for sponsorships to be greater than ever. They have no choice.

   When people ask me if I prefer things the way they were twenty years ago I answer honestly. No! I love NFL Football. It's more exciting than ever. The money issues are just part of our lives today. NFL Football is big business – bigger than ever. People who live in the past, who complain that nothing's as good as it used to be are diminishing the enjoyment of a sensational product. I choose to live in the present and I have no complaints.

This is a sales driven business. All air people should do everything they can to help sales. Account executives are often asking me to phone a prospective client and thank him or her for being interested in the broadcast. I'm always available to spend time with clients at lunch or meet them for a round of golf. This is all part of the business.

Early in your career you may be offered the opportunity to supplement your income at a small station by selling time when you're not on the air. Give it a try. You may like it. Even if it turns out to be something that is alien to your nature it will give you a feeling of what the sales department goes through. I've found that by developing a good relationship with the sales department it helps the entire atmosphere of the football operation. Another benefit is that these sales people may also go out of their way to get you involved as a spokesperson for one of their clients. This can make a major impact on your income. If you have a solid relationship with the sales people they are also more likely to listen to you when you believe a certain promotion is out of line. Mutual respect is a great thing.

THE FINAL GUN

I sincerely hope that this book has given you a wide-ranging view of what sportscasting is all about. As I've said repeatedly, it isn't an easy goal to achieve. But if you're driven, resilient, dedicated, determined, and relentless in your pursuit it is possible. If you are able to turn your passion into a profession there's nothing like it.

I wish you every success in the world!

ACKNOWLEDGEMENTS:

Elliott Alexander
Paul Baroli
Andy Bloom
Derek Boyko
Tom Cardella
Steve Cave
Skip Clayton
Stephanie Coons
Wendy Coons
Erica Darragh
Pat T. Deon Sr.
Jim Foxwell
Frank Gumienny
Larry Kane
Lew Klein
Joseph A. McPeak
Mike Quick
Marc Rayfield
Bill Rednor
Lloyd Zane Remick, Esq.
Al Shrier
Terry Small
Sue Smith
Steve Wanczyk
Joe Weachter
Cindy Webster
Dan Wing

Cover Photograph: Robert Rathe
Printing: Digital Color Graphics
Design: Jennifer Harrelson-Balasa

NOTES